C. J. Creed, Printer, Broadoak, Bridport

"IT'S AUTUMN NOW"

B. D. L. Festival 1939

the author as Elliston Drury

With Best Wishes

Fred. B. Alcock

AS IT WAS

FRED B. ALCOCK

Published by Amateur Players of Sherborne

Distributed by

The Abbey Bookshop, Sherborne, Dorset.

ACKNOWLEDGEMENTS

I am most grateful to many friends for their help and encouragement in compiling this story and for their active support in publishing it. In particular:—

Bewsey B. Dyke, Esq. J.P.
Donald A. Mildenhall, Esq.
Mrs. Margery Morgan
David Webb, Esq.
Mervyn G. Davies, Esq.
Major H. B. Watson, T.D. 1/5 Queen's Royal Regt.
Gerald Pitman, Esq.
S. T. Hyde, Esq.
John Bennett, Esq.
The Proprietors of The Western Gazette

I am indebted to the Trustees of the Theatre Royal, Bristol for permission to quote from "The Story of the Theatre Royal".

My sincere thanks also to my wife for all her hard work and great patience in making the original typescript.

THE ILLUSTRATIONS

The Cover Design is by Miss Claire Farley of A.P.S.

Most of the photographs, more than 30 years old and some nearly 50, are by the late A. R. Chaffin and are reproduced with the kind assistance of Mr. David Hunt.

The WARTIME VARIETY pictures are by the late A. G. Harris.

The THEATRE ROYAL photograph is reproduced by kind permission of Mr. Derek Balmer.

The Frontispiece is a "self portrait".

FRED. B. ALCOCK, 1978.

To
Joy Saunders

CHAIRMAN

AMATEUR PLAYERS OF SHERBORNE

ON THEIR

FORTIETH ANNIVERSARY

CONTENTS

FOREWORD
by Gerald H. D. Pitman

The curtain rises on a beautiful Dorset town towards the end of the 1920's. Enter a junior bank clerk and his loved one—the Theatre. A marriage is happily arranged and his company "Amateur Players of Sherborne" is born.

"As It Was" is the story of A.P.S. told by Frederick B. Alcock—or "Fred" as he is invariably referred to by so very many; in itself an expression of the remarkable affection felt by the "children" of the marriage. First let some of the "boys and girls" say for themselves how they feel about this gifted and strongly individualistic Player.

"When Fred came in 1927 I am not sure whether Sherborne adopted him or he adopted Sherborne! In everyone's life there are "magic moments" and I believe these pre-war years to be Fred's. I am grateful he has found the time to take this peep over his scraggy old shoulder and write down what he sees"—Ralph Hamblin.

" . . . . It was my great good fortune to know him, to work for him, to act with him, from the old days of the Operatic Society and his great Ko-Ko, right up to the time of our award-winning appearance at Bristol Theatre Royal in "Dear Brutus". What more could any amateur desire?" —Margery B. Morgan (neé Hall).

"When in 1930 the newly formed Sherborne Operatic and Dramatic Society decided to produce "The Mikado", a number of members had doubts about the choice of Fred Alcock to play Ko-Ko. How wrong they were!" Marjorie L. Burton (Yum-Yum).

"As our director he knew every branch of play production, acting, set construction and stage lighting. He knew exactly what he wanted and how to gain warm collaboration. The pleasure which A.P.S. have given to so many audiences over the year owes much to his early, unselfish and inspiring leadership"—Meg. and Ernest Hulme.

"I first met Fred at his most disarming. "We shall get on splendidly— if you do **exactly** as I say". How right he was! His tremendously high standard, hard work and precision brought results enjoyed as much by us as by the audiences, and that is saying a lot! Thanks for the memories, Fred." —Elizabeth Southcombe.

"An Arch Dictator, when these were fashionable, he achieved splendid results. We were bullied, but reasonably benevolently. "Remember, Boys and Girls, you are not here for your own amusement. A lot of people are paying good money to see this." At times we were lambasted in a way which, today, would result in "Industrial Action", but we sat up and asked for more!—Bewsey Dyke.

" . . . . A dual personality to whom the Illusion of the Theatre was real life and yet a shrewd businessman who achieved a notable career in Banking. Fred possessed the gift of inspiring fellow players with enthusiasm. His patience, skill and kindly persuasion gave confidence to many a young Player"—Mervyn Davies.

After leaving Sherborne, Fred worked in the 1950's for Belmont Players with Sydney T. Hyde, formerly Publicity Manager, W. H. Smith & Sons Ltd. and subsequently Chairman and Managing Director, W H S Advertising Ltd. Mr. Hyde, whose life has always been concerned directly with books, has written to the author — "It sounds trite and is one of the world's worst cliches, but the truth is that I couldn't put your book down. To me it is intensely interesting for, perhaps you may think, the wrong reasons— it gave me a very clear insight into you. Of course at Belmont we saw only the finished artist, not knowing how he had been shaped and fired, and it is fascinating to trace the development of your ways, your convictions, your fierce enthusiasms and your almost arrogant but carefully concealed insistence on getting your own way. You always looked for perfection, refused ever to be satisfied, or even allow yourself to enjoy your success.

Your book tells me so much I did not know about you, yet so much is endorsed that I had only suspected. The style is your own and your personality is stamped on every page. It is a book about Sherborne but you have also a splendid story about producing plays, running a theatre group and so on. It could be a real help to societies and an inspiration to producers in particular.

Above all, the qualities, the quirks, the honesty of this man Fred B. Alcock do come through."

Interested?   Intrigued?

The scene is set.

"Beginners Please."

GERALD H. D. PITMAN (Past Chairman A.P.S.)

CHAPTER ONE

IN THE BEGINNING

An evening in early summer 1934. Overhead, Alan Cobham's Air Circus roared its way triumphantly through a clear sky, having drawn all Sherborne, it seemed, to Bown's Field in Yeovil Road. In the Church Hall, less audible at times and certainly engaging less attention, an earnest band of amateur actors played "Rope" to an audience of about seventy people.

The stage was a temporary platform erected in front of the 'band-stand' alcove at one end of the hall, a sort of jetty which did not extend to the side-walls. There was no proscenium, the stage being bounded by green baize curtains suspended from a timber frame-work about twelve feet high. Wing space was at most three feet, but there was adequate depth into the alcove.

Impossible, one would have thought, yet upon this platform Maurice Welcher had produced "The Ghost Train" with great success for the Old Fosterians' Dramatic Society, then Sherborne's only theatre group with a continuing existence, and it was largely due to his ingenuity that "Rope" was now presented acceptably under the direction of R. G. Nicholls, (Manager of the National Provincial Bank) on behalf of the Abbey Men's Guild. Both Welcher and Ernest Hulme, from Old Fosterians, were in the cast. Others had been recruited from various recent casual productions: Peggy Merrick, who had recently come to Sherborne from "The Dorchester Follies"; Hugh Sawtell, who with friends had staged "Nothing But The Truth"; Mrs. A. J. P. Andrews and Fred Alcock who with R. G. Nicholls had been the only townsfolk in an otherwise School Staff performance of "She Passed Through Lorraine" at the School Gym in aid of the Lady Chapel Fund.

It was a scratch cast in a scratch show, working in wretched conditions to a wretchedly small audience. And it deserved better. Much genuine enthusiasm, months of preparation and at least a little talent had been devoted to that play and the end product was a good piece of theatre— thrown away for want of adequate presentation and publicity. So thought one of the company at least, a bank clerk playing the drunken Granillo. To him, it was all such a depressing waste of effort.

Unnecessary too, for Sherborne had a fine new theatre where the play could have seen justice done to it. The Operatic Society had packed it for Gilbert and Sullivan three years following, before collapsing for want of funds. And the same bank clerk thought that was a depressing waste too— of money.

In Act II, the drunken Granillo had a long wait off. On return, his confederate, played by Ernest Hulme, would bolster up his courage with the line, "Pull yourself together. Here drink this." It was meant to be a tot of whisky. In fact it was "Vimto"—Seymours' most highly aerated product. And it was not a tot, but a huge tumbler which Ernest, with his own brand of humour, had filled to the brim well knowing that Granillo's next line after tossing it back (as if that were possible) would be, "That's better, give me another of those." Which he did. It was disastrous. Ernest Hulme never fails.

But during the wait an idea had taken shape. Sitting on the stone steps outside the back door of the Church Hall, watching the aeroplanes still noisily cavorting overhead, Granillo had been thinking.

'There must be a better way. A big show entails no more effort than a small one. Here we are in "Rope", with a good play, working hard for a cause, but making a pitiful sum to carry out our intention. Yet, at The Carlton we take a lot of money, with no intention of helping anyone, only of enjoying ourselves and spending it. Both are wrong.'

'I know what I want. I want to try, however ineffectively, to bring a professional approach to an amateur show. A commercial approach, on as big a scale as, possible, to make as much money as possible for someone. Then we can get nearer the real thing. Then we can get rid of self-indulgent "pastime" acting and aim at something worthy of the word "theatre".

'Such an approach demands independent control. No subscriptions entitling "members" to elect representatives for policy making. It demands freedom in choice of play, in casting and in method of preparation. Above all it demands a company who will work as if their livelihood depends on it. It is too much to expect, obviously, but it can be the goal.'

'Given all that and a good theatre, a popular play and an appealing object we can achieve something—a professional job by amateurs. I know it can be done and I ask no better support than from those around me in "Rope". So let's take The Carlton, find someone to work for and Do a Play —my way.'

It was more than an idea. It was a resolve.

Then back to Act II, Ernest and "Vimto".

Forty years later I do not in any way defend this kind of approach. I want only to record what happened and what prompted events, right or wrong.

CHAPTER TWO

FRED B.

First person singular. It is unavoidable. It would be like trying to trace the course of a river without knowing its source. So, with apologies and a promise to keep to the mainstream, here goes:—

It all started for me when I was nine or ten and at Salisbury Cathedral School. I had been, I believe, a rickety babe and was certainly a timid weakling of a boy. Any self-confidence I had was shattered on the break-up of my home when I was eight. I was parted from Mother who was left in dreadful poverty to bring up my younger brother as best she could. My Father, before emigrating to Canada, put me in the charge of an elderly parson Uncle whom I feared and disliked. Thus it was a very poor little specimen who appeared in his sailor suit for a voice test at Salisbury in 1913. I was nicknamed Skinny at once—the reason was all too obvious— and my inability at games only served to increase my loneliness and misery. They were dark days, never forgotten.

Then Providence must have taken a hand. I suddenly discovered that I could make others laugh. Not at me, but with me. I could entertain. My "Dormy Shows" were my salvation. At last I was someone. There was something I could do better than others could, and I grasped it.

We had to stay at school over Christmas and that meant parties, plays and entertainments. To my joy I was singled out from the juniors to take comic parts, and by the time I was twelve I was "directing" boys much older than I. At fourteen came my first full play. My friend, one Ellison, had an elder brother at S.E.S. Oxford who had produced "A Christmas Carol" there. And what he could do, we could! It took us two terms to "dramatize" the story and we produced it for "the friends of the School" during the following Christmas. Ellison played Scrooge; I played all four ghosts!

Holidays, short though they were, proved difficult for my guardian, and I was bundled about a good deal amongst family friends. On one such a visit to Bournemouth came the treat that was to affect me more than any other entertainment I have ever attended. I was fifteen and it was my first G. & S. Opera — indeed it was my first "musical" — D'Oyly Carte, "The Mikado". I was enraptured. Here for me was the perfect combination of music and humour. I identified myself immediately with Ko Ko and dreamed and dreamed of playing him one day. I was given a libretto and learnt the part just to pretend. Henry Lytton was my hero and when I found that he appeared on the programme as Henry A. Lytton I became Fred. B. Alcock —on all school essays, letters and everything else. And Fred. B. I have remained ever since.

Later that same year—1920—I moved on to Shaftesbury Grammar School, as did two others from Salisbury, with the result that my nickname travelled with me. So did my reputation as a comedian. Here luck was really with me, for I was put in Ramshawe's house and Ramshawe had for years organised and supervised the School end-of-term entertainments.

I owe much to Mr. Ramshawe. From him I received my first real tuition in the disciplines of stagecraft. He found me good material for character sketches and monologues, and taught me the elements of stage-management and improvisation. I eventually became his assistant producer for the ambitious Christmas 1921 show and he somehow allowed me to feel that its success was mine. Looking back, I now recognise that by encouraging me to do what I could do well, and not to worry about my physical shortcomings and lack of sporting prowess, he did more to give me a confident start in the world than any other person responsible for my upbringing.

Thus it was that when at the age of sixteen I was inflicted upon Lloyds Bank in Bath, I was much better equipped for a career as an entertainer than in finance. And just as well, for my salary was £65 a year and my digs cost 19/- a week. Moreover Uncle had made it very clear that I was expected to maintain myself within twelve months.

I lost no time. Before I was eighteen I was earning quite good money as an after-dinner entertainer, at smoking concerts, etc., and from artists I met in this way, I formed a Costume Concert Party. It was good experience, no doubt, but a ghastly failure, which ended abruptly in a cinema at Bradford on Avon, when I could not pay the company. I was much younger than any of them and they were really very kind about it.

Meanwhile my education continued. First call on my funds was my Tuesday night at Bath's Theatre Royal. Then 1/6d. in the Pit (2/- early doors). "Sit close together please—every seat wanted". I nearly always went alone and almost every week. Bath was a No. 2 Touring date, but sometimes we got the No. 1 companies. And what a wonderful world I discovered. I was utterly uncritical, and made no distinctions. I just wanted to be there. The Shakespeareans, Frank Benson and Henry Baynton with their own companies: the new farces, "It pays to Advertise", "Tons of Money"; D'Oyly Carte (2nd Company); The Co-Optimists; the trail-blazer musical "No No Nanette"—I went twice to that. Then in the summer we had repertory from Lena Ashwell Players and Pelican Players. Going every week then, seeing the same actors in a variety of parts was an education indeed. I wanted intensely to be able to do that. A new part every week!

I also wanted more money—and made it in a dance band. I was now nineteen and for nearly two years I had been learning to play the banjo from one of the best old finger-style exponents in the World, Dick Tarrant-Bailey. That is a story in itself, but I must keep to the mainstream. Suffice now that, tempted by the arrival of the jazz-band era I formed a band with Arthur Clark, of Milsoms Music Shop who, although not a very good drummer had good connections in the field and was in the right position to obtain engagements. We recruited experienced men and had to pay them more than we got for ourselves, but it paid off. Within twelve months Arthur had a contract and we were "The Pump Room Dance Orchestra". He kept it going with great success for many years, but not, as it happens, with me.

It was 1926. I was 21. Doris, a steadying influence, much needed, had been talking for some time of a home of our own. Things were fine. Somehow I managed to hold my job in the Bank and that winter, with concert engagements and the band, we were quite well off.

Then came disaster! The Bank did not fire me as I certainly deserved, for I was acknowledged to be the worst junior ever suffered in Bath. Instead they transferred me to Sherborne.

CHAPTER THREE

BANK CLERK WITH A BANJO

It was a nervous and despondent junior bank clerk who stepped from the train on 23rd May 1927. Married for only eight months, I had lost the source of income which had enabled me to make ends meet and the Bank had duly warned me that if I got into financial difficulties through an early marriage I should get no sympathy; I should get the sack.

But if I was gloomy on that sunny May morning, Sherborne certainly was not. I was greeted by a gaily decorated Pageant Gardens, flags and bunting up and down Cheap Street and elaborate shop window displays. It was "Shopping Week", the climax of which was to be Charles Greenham's Donkey Derby which attracted thousands to the Castle Grounds to see the Country's leading jockeys.

One event advertised in connection with the Week took place after it was over. "A Grand Concert" at the Digby Assembly Rooms and it was to this that I owed my financial salvation. Desperate to establish myself as an entertainer and banjoist I approached the organiser, Sydney Waller, a local tenor (and Manager of Eldridge Popes) and was accepted, I suspect, only because it would be a new face in a company of very familiar performers. So although my first week at Lloyds Bank, Sherborne had been pretty depressing for everyone I felt happier on returning from the weekend in Bath to have with me my music, gear for my act and my banjo, and went to meet my accompanist for the concert, Jessie Brown who would be appearing. of course, with her husband W. J. E. (Bill) Brown, Dorset Dialect Comedian. Thus started a warm friendship that was to last for the remainder of their lives.

Maybe Bill kept his yokel act going a little too late into old age, but in 1927 he could top the bill in good company. I greatly admired him as a gifted comedian. He was a good character actor too and his gentle "Mr. Pym" lived on in memory long after an undistinguished production of the play in Long Street Schoolroom. It was a memory that was to serve me well when I needed a Coady for "Dear Brutus" nearly twenty years later. Bill and Jessie were to do great work for the Players and I know that our company meant much to them. It is touching that after "Mr. Pym" had finally passed by, Bill had made a bequest to Amateur Players of Sherborne "in memory of Jessie".

But at that first Sherborne Concert it was another act which seized my urgent attention. Billed as "On Stage" were "The Blackmore Vale Orchestra under the direction of P. J. Shaw L.R.A.M.". They were a nine piece dance band, smart in their scarlet dinner-jackets, and good. Their pianist Wilby Shaw was really brilliant in his young days, certainly the best dance player I have known, even though he scarcely knew what a sharp sign meant. Little did I realise that no small part of the impact made by "No No Nanette" some eight years later would be due to Wilby and his brother, or that the whole show would depend on the two little girls at present eight years old whose dancing with the band was the high-spot of the act. They were Jack Shaw's twin daughters, Pat and Betty who even at that age brought a professional precision (and perhaps a natural telepathy) to their quite complicated routines which earned them a great reception.

However, it was not the performance of the band which sent my heart leaping, but an obvious gap in their rhythm section. They had no banjoist. Within a week Grandad Shaw (the only tailor I have ever seen who sat cross-legged on the table to sew) had altered a red dinner jacket to fit me and I was playing with the B.V.O. at Yeovil. So started two years of close association with some of the best friends ever. The leader (violin) was Freddie Bunce (Cole, Jeweller, The Parade); alto sax Doug Philpott (Min. of Labour); myself banjo and guitar (I tuned the latter like a banjo!); Piano, Wilby Shaw; Drums, Vic Stevens (Shaw's piano tuner). This was the small band. the same combination as the famous Kettner Five whom we tried to emulate. Next came the brass: the astonishing young "Nippy" Crouch, trumpeter and that great character Charlie Parsons (Trombone), whose lifetime of work for the Sherborne Boys Brigade was later recognised with an O.B.E. For the big occasions we imported from Bournemouth Vic's brother Jim on tenor sax and "Mac" Macdonald playing a second piano. Jack Shaw himself appeared sometimes to play a Sousaphone.

The band was in demand over a wide area of the West Country. There were long journeys to Hunt Balls at Barnstaple and Tiverton; nearer home at Taunton and Bridgwater; and the smaller but lucrative Saturday Pops some of which we ran ourselves. Hard work, at the wrong end of the day, but it was good fun with good friends, and for me a great stroke of luck. Once again my banjo paid me more than the Bank, and Doris and I, renting a cottage in Hound Street could now prepare with confidence to welcome Joy.

Once established, I gave banjo lessons and in one of my earliest pupils I found a firm young friend who, with his family, did so much to make us happy and at home in Sherborne. Years later John Elliott was to be Amateur Players' first stage manager.

A whole book could be written about the Elliotts—"J. H. & G. Elliott, Cabinet Makers, Antique Furniture Restorers". Indeed it is said that H. A. Vachell wrote "Quinnies" after acquainting himself with their workshops in Newland. They supplied some of the furnishings for the first production of that famous play.

The family had come to Sherborne originally to do work on the restoration of the Abbey, their first workshops being on the site of the Yeatman

Hospital Many tales are told of their "reproductions" of antique furniture.

Uncle George, a bachelor, headed the firm when I first knew the family He was a great character and a fine craftsman who had numbered Charles Dickens amongst his friends. Aunt Rose managed the antique shop. She was considered one of the cleverest china repairers in the country doing work for the top sales-rooms and dealers. J. H. Elliott had died before we came to Sherborne and it was his widow who was so kind to Doris and me when Joy was a baby. Her children, Muriel, John and George were all to be connected with the first production of Amateur Players years later and to Muriel goes the distinction of having spoken the very first line in our history—"Any News Mr. Sprules"

It was John who, in 1928, gave me the news, a whisper only, that next to the Elliott's property in Newland, Mr. Rowland Reeves, who owned the cinema in Cheap Street, intended to build a fine new theatre for Sherborne.

CHAPTER FOUR

"WESSEX"—"CARLTON"

Fine and new it was—a little gem of a theatre. Seating five hundred and forty in comfort; well furnished, possessing foyer and adequate cloak-rooms, it was equipped with first class machines for the projection of—tragically—silent films. It was said that Rowland Reeves had sunk all he possessed in the theatre and when progress demanded "talkies" there was simply no money left for the conversion. Too late came offers of finanical help from local businessmen and the theatre passed into the hands of a Mr. Carter and Mr. Pilkington who owned, individually, other cinemas in the area. Combining their surnames they found a new name for theatre, —hence "Carlton".

But we first knew it under the public-spirited ownership of Mr. Reeves —as "The Wessex".

The proscenium was of handsome proportions, with a 24ft. opening. It was high; we used 18ft. flats. The flat stage was 18ft. deep with a passage behind from one side to the other, off which opened four dressing rooms. Below stage were two larger dressing rooms and the (very popular) boiler room, which also served as "green room" and bar!

Stage lighting was good by the standards of the time. It was installed by D.C. Electric (Jimmy Dootson) and comprised three-colour battens and floats, spots in the perches and F.O.H., all adequately dimmed from a not very flexible switchboard.

Acoustics were perfect: a whisper really could be heard "bouncing off the back wall". A gem of a theatre.

CHAPTER FIVE

KO — KO

G. W. Fox, Manager of Lloyds Bank, was about the last man in Sherborne, I would have thought, to take a practical interest in the new theatre. I was wrong, as I found out during an uncomfortable interview.

I had been carpeted for falling asleep in the office. For this there was some excuse, since from 9 p.m. to 3 a.m. I had been playing the banjo in Barnstaple. And that was the end of my dance band career. Mr. Fox had certainly known and disapproved of it, but had generously turned a blind eye as long as he could, so that I might avoid financial troubles. It was typical of him that, now the time had come to put an end to it, his principal objection was not that I failed to do my job or that I fell asleep in the office, but that a member of the staff should be a paid performer on the platform when his colleagues were guests at a dance. Mr. Fox never walked up Cheap Street without carrying his gloves.

On the other hand he had encouraged my concert work and had indeed introduced me to appear for his friends who were organising entertainments, notably the Southcombes of Milborne Port. So it was not surprising that he wound up the interview, which he had found as embarrassing as I, by telling me that he would expect me, of course, to join the new Operatic Society to be formed. This was the first I had heard of it, and what did surprise me was that it was he who was forming it. But yes, as I now know, the idea was born in George Fox's drawing room in conversation with a new friend, a young doctor who had come to join Dr. MacCarthy, Richmond McIntosh.

Dr. McIntosh had some experience in "G. & S." and the confidence to undertake the production of—to my great excitement when I heard of it—"The Mikado". Mr. Fox had, on the books of Lloyds Bank, the remaining funds of a defunct choral society which led him to Alf Lowman, Harold Dodge and others of its late membership. Next, to the School and its Director of Music B. J. F. Picton who agreed to accept the same office for the Operatic Society. An inaugural meeting was held on 14th October 1929 and the Society was launched.

C. L. F. Boughey, Headmaster, permitted the use of the Music School for rehearsals and several of the School staff took part. At once Picton, a strong personality in authority in his own schoolroom and a master musician, absolutely dominated the production both at rehearsal and in the committee room. He probably made Dr. McIntosh's task far from simple and his insistence on nothing but the best in professional musicians, scenery and costumes caused anxiety to the Treasurer, Mr. Fox.

I was hesitant, to say the least. From the age of fifteen—I was then twenty-four—I had dreamed of playing "Ko Ko", but the probability of my being given the chance seemed too remote to contemplate. I felt socially inferior: after all, schoolmasters, doctors, bank managers, balding businessmen were far removed from the standing of an impecunious junior clerk and dance-band player. But my friends Bill and Jessie Brown were going to join, so was Jack Shaw, and, a deciding factor, George Fox "expected" it of me. So I found myself amongst the second tenors, feeling nervous every time I approached the Music School and ill at ease sitting there holding a score in my lap.

There were no auditions for parts. I learned later that in committee it was decided to approach various members and that Mr. Fox had put my name forward as a possible "Ko-Ko". In the event, he himself under-studied the part and, I suspect, he may have been offered it. At the time all that happened was that one night, as we were singing the chorus leading to Ko-Ko's entrance, Picton called "Alcock, try it"—"Taken from the County Jail"—I cannot describe the leap of joy, the stab of fear I felt as I stumbled through the song. I knew it. I had imagined myself singing it over and over again in fantasy. Yet it was a dismal effort.

Picton, however, did not ask anyone else to take it and just as we were leaving he told me I would read Ko-Ko at the first dialogue rehearsal and sing the "Little List" song. I was scared, of course, but at the end of the song there were a few handclaps from the company and from then on it was easy. I felt a strong affinity with the cheap tailor from Titipu, saddled with responsibilities much too big for him, trying to keep his end up amongst all the high dignitaries of State, and as the production took shape I lived deeper and deeper in the part, thinking of little else.

We built up, I believe, a good standard of performance. Marjorie Lowman was a delightful little Yum-Yum. Hugh Elder, from the School, a splendidly impressive Pooh-Bah. Nanki-Poo, the "second trombone" wandering minstrel was played by, of all people, Vernon House, the teacher of wind instruments at the School! Richmond McIntosh, as well as producing, was The Mikado. The only future Amateur Player, apart from me, in the principals was Doris's young friend, Dulcie Hunt as Peep-Bo. Her little brother David was Ko-Ko's sword bearer.

The opera was performed at The Wessex Theatre for three days from 20th March 1930. From the outset, Mr. Fox aimed to make it the biggest social event in Sherborne for years, and to this end we had the Squire, Col. Wingfield-Digby for President, supported by seventeen distinguished Vice-Presidents and no less than one hundred and twenty Honorary Members, who got some free seats and their names in the programme. There were Special Patrons on each night. Everyone was there who should be there and all agreed it was a great success. After the final performance there were endless bouquets and presentations and congratulations.

So far as I know, we did give a good show, due mostly to the talented musicianship and command of B. J. F. Picton, for whom I had a great respect and admiration as a musical director, but it must be confessed with shame that my only interest was entirely selfish. I just wanted my Ko-Ko to be a hit, the hit. And I was well pleased with my reception, taking much too much credit for myself and allowing too little to Messrs. G. and S. A lesson yet to be learnt.

I did learn something from it though. To me, the only purpose of the show had been a hollow one—the pastime and amusement of those taking part. And to me that was—is—wrong. I had revelled in my success in a part I had longed to play for nine years and it ought to have been the realisation of a dream, but I did miss some sense of achievement without quite knowing why. This vague feeling of discontent with the "tennis club" aspect of amateur theatre was to grow and clarify during the next four years, finally finding expression in the formation of a company—not a society—to produce plays with more objective than mere self-gratification.

What happened next was not only to bring me probably the most exciting week of my whole life, but would have a strong bearing upon the path that company was to follow during its early years.

Just before Easter and three weeks after our opera, an urgent appeal came from Taunton Operatic Society. They were to produce "The Mikado" during the week after Easter week and their Ko-Ko had fallen ill. Their Secretary, Sidney Ward, had seen our show and it was decided to approach me rather than seek a professional whom they had not seen.

I turned at once to George Fox, who promptly took charge. Yes, I could go. No, I could not have a week off, or take part of my holiday. I must travel each day, but I could leave work at 4.30 p.m. (12 noon on matinée days) and he would arrange transport. Yes, I could have Easter Saturday off for rehearsal.

Taunton Operatic Society, founded in 1905, was a very strong and influential body, and, I believe, it is so today. All that I have said about the Sherborne Society may be multiplied, with the added quality of long tradition. Taunton Opera Week was quite an occasion. But this time I had no reservations. This was different. This time I was an actor, with an urgent job to do, on my own in strange company. And it was great.

The producer and musical director was Avalon Collard, an elderly martinet who claimed to have known both W. S. Gilbert and Arthur Sullivan. He had advised the engagement of a professional to play Ko-Ko and he certainly cast a very sceptical eye upon me, insisting that he would have to teach me the part from scratch. I hated it and him, but it did me good.

I spent all Good Friday and Easter Sunday on the empty stage of the Lyceum Theatre with relays of pianists and Mr. Collard playing all the other parts, but I did not meet the cast until the following weekend for my only two rehearsals. Then I made a bad start. Rushing on nervously with the line, "Ah, my bride that is to be" I kissed the wrong girl! My obvious confusion melted any reserve there had been and from then on there was such an air of warmth and welcome that I knew I could not fail. Not only were these new friends wonderfully helpful but they seemed to have confidence in me.

Of the week itself, modesty ought to forbid, but—Yes, I was happy. The local Press had made much of the young actor travelling thirty miles from Sherborne each day to fill the breach. The first night audience, curious at first, warmed to a most generous response and the congratulations did flatter me. I must admit my pleasure at a nice little notice in the Daily Mail, no less, headed "Amateur Success by Understudy". The Chronicle too. As the run progressed, so did my joy in the part and in my reception. For me, this was the real thing, my boyhood dream come true. My performance would not have withstood expert criticism I am sure, but as I made my entry on the last night the applause which greeted me would have satisfied the great Lytton himself. Even Avalon Collard smiled to me across the orchestra pit as he waited, baton poised; and as I made my little bow of acknowledgement I knew a moment of complete and total fulfilment. It comes once in a lifetime, they say.

CHAPTER SIX

SIGNPOSTS

The year, 1931—feet on the ground again, but firmer and more self-assured now. The Taunton adventure had brought me, in addition to many good friends there for years ahead, quite a bit of improved standing locally. I was no longer nervous on approaching the Music School to rehearse; this time, "Iolanthe".

The show followed much the pattern of that of the previous year. Marjorie Lowman, Vernon House, Hugh Elder and I were again amongst the principals. Dr. McIntosh again produced, though this time with the help at the final rehearsals of a well-known professional, Richard Andean. This was not the only extra expense; Picton wanted, and got an even bigger and better band and the new owners of the theatre, now The Carlton, were demanding much tougher terms. Despite all George Fox's efforts in drumming up more Vice-Presidents and Honorary Members we had difficulty in making ends meet, which considering the money we took, quite upset me!

The performances went very well, with better polish it was said, than we had shown in "The Mikado". I greatly enjoyed playing the Lord Chancellor, feeling at ease and assured in the part, and I think we all found the show good fun.

Beforehand though, the season had not gone very smoothly. There were clashes of personality and we heard of "words" in the committee room. All too frequently we arrived to rehearse only to find the chairs facing the wrong way because there was to be a meeting of members instead. I found these meetings very trying to the patience. The formal procedure seemed so silly and dull and to my mind had no place in a theatrical production. The stupidest suggestions were adopted on a show of hands belonging to people who had not the slightest idea of the problem in mind, only to be withdrawn at a later meeting called specially for the purpose because they were found to be unworkable. I became utterly convinced that all this giving expression to the wishes of fee-paying members may be right for a social club, but it is not the way to stage a play.

This, however was to concern me no longer, for I was not to appear again with the Operatic Society. I had been slowly coming to realise that as a family man I should start to take at least a little more interest in my job which, though still looked upon as pen-pushing, was getting a little less boring as I progressed. Repeatedly I had been warned that if I did not study for, and pass, the examinations of the Institute of Bankers I should get nowhere. But the exams were held annually in the Spring, which meant studying during the winter and that was when I had other thoughts to occupy me. So each year I had been fighting a losing battle with myself—

until 1932.

Then the Operatic Society decided to produce "Patience" and in this there was no part for me. I was the wrong shape for Bunthorne and could not sing it well enough. So that made up my mind. Jack Perham stepped in to play the part and I settled down to swot. (It took me six years to pass my Finals which explains why there were no spring productions for Amateur Players during their first years.)

* * * * *

Joy was now nearly five and started school at St. Antony's in September 1932. Amongst many happy new friendships we made there, none was to mean more to me than my meeting with another parent, Maurice Welcher, a senior master at Foster's School. I had seen his school productions of "Vice Versa" in the old school building and "Outward Bound" by The Old Fosterians' Society which he had staged under impossible conditions at the Digby (Hotel) Assembly Rooms.

I took to Maurice at once, which was surprising: to some he was rather a quiet, withdrawn figure—and anyway he was my senior by some years. Yet from the very start, in the warmth of our mutual enthusiasm for amateur theatre, we seemed to understand each other, and in the years to come we were to work closely together. I came to admire his ingenuity in improvisation of stage effects and his knack, when producing amateurs, of knowing how far to coach and when to leave matters to the actor. In the early years of the Players he greatly influenced their progress, whether as their first producer, or as actor, or indeed in plays with which he was not directly concerned, for even then I frequently sought his advice and many projects were re-shaped as a result.

Soon after we first met, Welcher undertook the ambitious task of producing "The Ghost Train" for the Old Fosterians. Ambitious because of its dependence upon elaborate sound and lighting effects and the complete lack of any facilities at the Church Hall. But with his home-made "drain-pipe" dimmers, biscuit-tin floods, magic lantern slides (for train windows) milk churn (for slamming carriage doors), a garden roller, and other wonderful "train" noises he achieved effects of much greater "presence" than any tape or disc reproduction, and far more fun for the crew! He had good backing from a hardworking cast and all went well.

My own modest involvement was that of helping George Elliott with the leading comedy role. This 1920's "silly ass" part did not come easily to him and we had to work quite hard in private. I went to rehearsals to watch results and here I met amongst the cast a number of those who were to be early Amateur Players. Ernest Hulme, Muriel Davis, Gwen Pine-Coffin, George Elliott, Gerald Brett and his sister Phyllis were all in the play. John Elliott was Stage Manager.

This production made a great impression on me. Looking back I think

I would say it gave me the first positive desire to form a company one day to present plays in the way I thought right. "The Ghost Train" was a good piece of theatre which could have pulled crowds to the Carlton had it been adequately publicised as an entertainment primarily for the public at large with the sole object of making money for someone. No doubt it attained its limited objective as a club show but to my mind that was not enough.

What did please me greatly though, and set me an example for the future was the decision to give an extra performance at Yetminster. Ever since my earliest concert-party days in Bath I had been keen on "fit-up" theatre. The challenge of setting up on different stages and playing to new audiences seemed to me to come just a step nearer professionalism, the real theatre. This little adventure was a great success, hugely enjoyed by everyone.

Piece by piece then, experience was pointing the road ahead. To get it right we must command large audiences and that meant The Carlton. The Operatic Society had taught me that the way to fill it was to create a social occasion. To support the play must be "the thing to do". It had also taught me what not to do. There would be no rule by elected committee, no membership, no "pastime" element and no expensive professional aids to eat up funds.

From "The Ghost Train" I had learnt the value and the satisfaction of making the whole show, scenery, props, effects, everything; exercising ingenuity in improvisation to keep down costs. I had admired the seriousness of purpose and the sense of urgency in rehearsals which Maurice Welcher had inspired in his quiet way. This, I felt, was the way to run a play, even if it was not the way to sell it.

Certainly though, the strongest influence in directing me was my earlier experience in entertaining for money, small as it had been—I firmly believed that by the simple device of aiming to take and make as much money as possible for someone — this to be the first consideration — all the other requisites for success would follow; the widest possible appeal, the best possible performances, the most efficient and economical organisation—in fact, the professional approach. As reward I saw in the achievement of giving the last possible penny to a chosen cause, something much more satisfying than "acting for fun". There was nothing altruistic in this, it was just my notion of how it should be.

And a notion it remained for a while. Then came "Rope" played to an audience of seventy with Alan Cobham's Air Circus overhead, and that made up my mind for me. I would have a go.

CHAPTER SEVEN

AMATEUR PLAYERS OF SHERBORNE

Pulling shut the door of Lloyds Bank after work I stood on the pavement undecided whether to go first up Cheap Street to see John Dingley, the Secretary of The Yeatman Hospital, or round the corner into Long Street and the N.P. to ask R. G. Nicholls to be Business Manager. I chose the latter and was told at once, "You could not have done better, I am Treasurer of the Yeatman Hospital". And from then on A.P.S. was no longer the child of just one man's imagination.

I put a definite plan to Mr. Nicholls. We would work for the Hospital: "Established 1866, supported by Voluntary Subscription" (—how that reflects the passage of time!). There was a big appeal effort in hand in connection with the new wing and I judged that the idea of supplementing the donations of the big guns by paying a modest sum for an acceptable entertainment would be popular with the townsfolk.

My search for the best possible "box-office" comedy that would be practicable was easy. This was the period of the famous Ralph Lynn, Tom Walls, Aldwych farces and "Tons of Money", the first of them was already an established favourite. I remembered it well from Bath Theatre Royal days and, to be honest, I selfishly relished the idea of playing the comedy lead.

Getting the Carlton would present no great problem. The Operatic Society had run out of steam, having produced nothing since 1932. (This may or may not have had something to do with Mr. Fox's retirement and departure in that year). A "live show" would, therefore, be welcome. Moreover, there had been a change in ownership: Mr. Pilkington had gone and his half share been bought by three local worthies, Messrs. Percy Coaker, Alan Seager and Jack Shaw, who I guessed (wrongly) would be eager to help a big charity show in their theatre.

Mr. Nicholls listened patiently as I poured out all my cherished ideas and theories, my enthusiasms and my prejudices, the right approach, the wrong approach: and when at last I stopped he quietly agreed to be Business Manager and then set about bringing me down to earth. Of course we must have a committee, or at least some sort of co-ordinating body and of course we could not contemplate such a large scale enterprise without any funds or guarantors. And so on. Even as he spoke I cast him as the family solicitor in "Tons of Money". Why had I never noticed that he looked like Robertson Hare?

There was no doubt about my hopes as to a producer, so my next call was upon Maurice Welcher. He too, heard me out. His face seemed to grow longer the more I went on. But I knew that was nothing to go by: Maurice was not given to displays of wild enthusiasm. Eventually he delivered himself of the view that in farce any producer is entirely in the hands of his comedians, but that he would "hold the book" if that is what I wanted, so long as he was not to be held responsible if no-one came to see us.

Then to Jack Shaw, in a tentative approach to the theatre. He, (and he alone, it transpired,) welcomed the idea and would consult his co-directors. And here I met the first snag. On being summoned to meet them I found my three local friends standing silent around the wall of the office whilst Mr. Carter made it perfectly clear from the chair that he held the cheque book—to use his own words. I had a very difficult time and came away with nothing better than 50% of the gross for a Monday, Tuesday and Wednesday, four performances in all and the Sunday for "get-in" and dress rehearsal. (There were no Sunday films in those days.) The 50% was a blow, because in order to avoid payment of a heavy Entertainment Tax, then in force, we had to give a minimum of 50% of the takings to charity and on this basis we should not have a penny for production costs.

But I had found a good Business Manager and the resourceful Ray Nicholls had the answer. Three in fact. We would appeal for Patrons, as the Operatic Society had done, but we would not give free seats. (Actually I had already agreed with Mr. Carter that there should be no free seats for anyone other than the Press.) Our appeal would be on the lines that by subscribing half a guinea towards our costs Patrons might enable us to give our total share of the takings to the Hospital. Secondly, in professional theatre manner, the cost of printing programmes would be paid for by advertisements and the nurses whom we hoped would sell them at the theatre could say that every penny paid for a programme would go to the Hospital. Lastly, the actors would pay all their own personal expenses. This was a great stroke, for it did not involve much sacrifice, it was good publicity and it got rid of the idea of "amateur theatricals" for the fun of the actors at the expense of the audience. In line with all this we must keep expenses down to the very minimum.

So we set the pattern for our future, although at the time we did not know there would be any. So also did we shape the system of co-ordination that was to work so smoothly through the years. It would be based on personal responsibility and involvement. The Committee (for want of a better name) would comprise only those in charge of the various aspects of our project, plus two from the benefiting charity. Its function would be confined to checking and co-ordinating work-in-progress and we reckoned to meet only two or three times. There would be no committee decisions because the original concept of one-man control would apply not only to general strategy but to every department, and once an office had been undertaken the holder really would be in charge and responsible for results. Right or wrong, I believed and I still do, that two heads may be better than one in many matters, but not in the theatre.

So now I set about recruiting. Welcher had almost cast the play to his satisfaction from the "Ghost Train" and "Rope" companies and I called on each choice in turn, expounding my ideas and ambitions for the kind of show, scale of production and so on over and over again, trying to make attractive the prospect of a short but very heavy schedule of rehearsals, working for a nondescript organisation and, in the end, paying one's own expenses. And I must say I was amazed at the eager response: not one turned me down. I like to think my own, almost fanatical, enthusiasm may have proved infectious, or it may have been the attraction of playing on a permanent stage to a theatre audience for the first time. Whatever it was, Maurice Welcher greeted a band of keen, willing workers when we met for our first rehearsal in a small room in Abbey Road early in October.

Two parts had remained to be filled. For one I cast Queenie South-combe on the spur of the moment when she happened to come in to the Bank one day. We had done some concerts together in the past, she looked right for the part and I admit to thinking her influence in Milborne Port would be good for the box-office. It was not a proper way to allot a part but, in the event Queenie more than justified the choice. The other part seemed made for W. J. Cordy, a friend and old colleague of Mr. Nicholls, who had come recently to Sherborne and South Western Dairies. Mr. Cordy was not young then, but remained a good friend of the Players for many years and eventually became their first President.

With rehearsals under way and the theatre booked it was time to attend to mounting and selling the show. John Elliott stepped naturally into his rightful job as Stage Manager, almost without a word, and we decided at once to hire the cheapest set we could and make it look as good as possible with careful lighting and striking furniture. (By curious coincidence we hired the very set in which I had been photographed with the Blackmore Vale Band years earlier at Knightstone Pavilion, Weston-super-Mare, where it had done service the night before).

To complete our organisation we enlisted my Lloyds Bank colleague, George Merrick as Treasurer, an office I had thought unnecessary until the decision to invite Patrons, Hugh Sawtell (also in the cast), Printing and Advertising; Jack Shaw, Advance Booking and Box Office; W. J. Cordy, (cast) Patrons and Subscribers, with H. G. Dyer and W. A. T. Jarrett from the Hospital Committee.

We employed every device we could think of to build the show up into a social occasion. Shamelessly we worked on the assumption that you could stick posters up and down Cheap Street for ever and no one would take any notice, but get them to talk about the show over Afternoon Bridge in the Avenue and it was sold! In getting it known amongst the Right People we found Bank cashiers a great help. A little adroit name-dropping worked wonders. We invited the Matron and Staff of the Hospital to be our Special

Patrons on the opening night: The President of the Hospital, Col. Wingfield Digby on the second night. The Chairman and Members of the U.D.C. on the last night, and they all accepted.

I may not have been very proud of all our devious methods of persuading people to come to the theatre, but I was certainly relieved when I could see the idea was catching on, for I had been assailed by awful qualms at this stage. Maurice Welcher may have been right, and no-one would come to see us. Worse, I secretly felt everyone else was thinking the same! After all, we had absolutely no standing as a company and we were presenting the sort of entertainment that usually attracted two hundred or so to the Church Hall, whereas we needed to pull in two thousand in all. Memories of those grim Concert Party days in Bath were all too vivid: I had already known the misery of trying to make an empty house laugh whilst carrying the responsibility for the show. I was doing what I had wanted to do for so long in the way I had wanted, but I could not for the life of me think why.

Then Mr. Nicholls had his brainwave. He packed me off to the Carlton again to see how cheaply we could have it for an extra Private Performance on the Tuesday. This time I saw Mr. Carter alone and must have caught him in a weak moment, for he was quite jovial and expansive. He listened as I poured out my tale of our difficulties over the tax position and his 50%, and easily agreed to let us use the theatre, but without staff, for a nominal £5 to cover light and heat. Meanwhile Nicholls paid his second call upon the new Headmaster of Sherborne School, Mr. A. Ross-Wallace. Yes, the boys could come to a special performance at 5 p.m. on the Tuesday at 2/- each. Moreover this could be charged on the boys' bills. There was 100% acceptance and what an audience! Now we were sure of getting the Entertainment Tax back. Now also, we had some status. If the School was coming it must be the thing to do. The list of Patrons was growing and by the time booking opened we had the feel of success. But it was going to be hard work. Five shows in three days, and for me a long part with six costume changes.

Our "Committee" meeting, held about three weeks before the show, had an optimistic and confident air—except for me. I felt wildly excited and worried to death at the same time, a feeling I was to know over and over again in the years to come. But that is probably what it is all about.

The meeting did yield one good new suggestion from Jack Shaw. What about an orchestra? I ought to have thought of it before, for I have always felt that live music for overture and entr'actes does marvels for theatre atmosphere and the Carlton had an orchestra pit. The Sherborne and Thornford Orchestra, twenty-one strong, conducted by Mrs. Luxmoore agreed to come, and very pleasant music they provided. I am sure our entertainment would not have seemed so complete and nicely rounded off without them.

Hugh Sawtell was doing great things on publicity. He got the boys of Foster's School to decorate and man a splendid "Tons of Money" float in the Sherborne Carnival procession, conveniently held a week or so prior to our play. He organised a "Tons of Money" Dance to be held just after the play. Our costumes all had to be ready ten days early for a photo call at Reg Chaffin's studio and the results were displayed separately in various shop windows with appropriate captions. This worked well; shopkeepers were happier to accept a single card with photo rather than a large display, and window-shoppers looked more than once. We had the benefit, of course, of the theatre's normal poster advertising and slides on the screen, but this was restricted to one week for obvious reasons. By the time that came out, it was pretty well known that "Tons of Money" was "coming shortly".

Meanwhile, Maurice Welcher had put together a good show. It was fast, slick and well drilled. He worked us hard and strictly for just over six weeks, a concentrated effort which had nothing of staleness about it, although it must be admitted that we could find nothing funny in it by the day of the dress rehearsal.

In the event, I think we all acknowledged that the success which we certainly enjoyed was due largely to Maurie's disciplined production and the brilliant comedy of Peggy Merrick in the part that had been created years before by Yvonne Arnaud. Peggy was an astonishing girl. In everyday life she was an eccentric. She hid a pretty face behind a startling pink and white make-up, disguised a vivacious charm behind a show of irritating banter and almost invited one to criticize her every action, every speech, every intention. Yet she made and kept many good friends and her perpetually exasperated husband adored her. On stage we had to recognise her as that rare bird, a really talented light comedienne, with a gift for immediate rapport with an audience, an intuitive sense of timing and an infectious air of gaiety. Acting with her was a delight and whilst the laughs came my way, she made them for me skilfully and unselfishly. Sadly our happy partnership in "Tons of Money" was never to be repeated, but that is another story. In this one Peggy was our star.

We opened on Monday, 19th November, 1934 to a good house. My doubts about having to take the first part of the week had been unfounded and especially so in the case of the Wednesday (early closing) matinée which was full. So was the School performance, for Mr. Nicholls had persuaded Mr. Lindsay to let the Prep. School boys come too. I can recall no major catastrophes throughout the five shows and our reception was very generous, probably more so than we really deserved so far as standards went. But we did feel rewarded for the efforts we had put into the play, happy that, according to The Western Gazette's glowing account, about 1,850 people had seen the four public performances, happy at that sure sign of success—"unreserved seats full". Happy too, and why not, at the gales of laughter and the warmth of the response given us.

And efforts there had certainly been. Any of us would have found it hard to say just what had inspired the extra concentration, urgency and serious endeavour, but we were all aware of something special. Perhaps it was the occasion, the first play ever on a real stage in a real theatre in Sherborne, or the scale of production and size of audience, or Maurice Welcher's influence. Whatever it was, it worked and it was a very tired and very happy company that took the final line-up and listened to the cheers as Ray Nicholls stepped forward, not to pass up bouquets and presents, but to say simply that we hoped to give "nearly £100" to the Yeatman Hospital. In today's coinage that may not sound much but it was impressive in 1934 and everyone, company, orchestra, programme sellers, advertisers, audience, all could feel they had a part in that result. The final sum was £101.

Well, not quite the final sum; there was a further donation resulting from an extra private performance, and very hilarious it was, on a Sunday afternoon at St. Antony's Convent; an occasion still vividly remembered by the Reverened Mother forty years later. It is remembered also by one who, as a model little seven-year-old pupil, blushed in acute embarrassment that her father should appear amongst the nuns and all her friends, clad only in boat-cushions and a rudder.

By then, unfortunately, father was already feeling poorly. What ought to have been a simple cold developed into quite a severe return of bronchial trouble. It may have been just coincidnce, but Dr. Jack thought otherwise and said severe words to me. So I missed the "Tons of Money" Dance and celebrations, but the many folk who came to see me in bed left me in no doubt about the success we had enjoyed. And "enjoyed" is right; far more so than if we had set out with only our enjoyment in mind. We had found the formula for future efforts and we had forged warm friendships for life.

It was not until twelve months later when preparing the next production that we turned back to the "Tons of Money" programme to see how we had described ourselves. And there it was:—"Presented by Amateur Players of Sherborne". It was not a title, just a description meant to be modest, in the sense of "some amateur players", and, indeed, that is exactly how The Western Gazette reported the play—no capital letters even. But our name it became and there is none that has meant more to me in all my life.

CHAPTER EIGHT

NO, NO, NANETTE

Second daughter, Judy, joined the family in 1935, assisted by, amongst others, the Town Nurse, and as in so many others of her cases, our friendship with Nurse Powell continued long after her professional services were needed. Thus it was that one day when she was having tea with us, Doris commanded me: "you know we ought to do a show for the Town Nurse Fund", and in no time Nurse Powell had me taking to Miss Goodbody and Mrs. Jarrett who ran the Fund.

So much for the Cause, but the choice of show was decided by a number of unconnected factors all of which seemed to point in one direction:—

1. Last year's success with "Tons of Money" left a demand for a second show on the same lines.
2. The Operatic Society being still silent, there was a demand for a show with a large cast.
3. Taunton, with whom I kept in touch, were going modern and, under their new producer Eva Calabout, were updating "The Country Girl": (we heard tales of dancing and limbering classes from eight months before the show, even of early-morning training runs!)
4. Welcher introduced me to a new colleague of his at Foster's School, Geoffrey Hewitt, a musician who had previously conducted some G. & S. and was keen to "do a musical".
5. Jack Shaw's twin dancing daughters, just sixteen, were opening a "Blackmore Vale School of Dancing".

All this at about the time I read somewhere that "No, No, Nanette" was at last released for amateurs and was, in fact, to be produced at Brighton by Harry Drury, a professional I had met (for some years he produced for Gillingham Operatic Society).

Why not? It would be something entirely new for Sherborne and for miles around. I had some experience in a song and dance show as a concert party comedian. I had a possible musical director and two dancing teachers; there was the Blackmore Vale Band. Again it was Doris who urged me on, persuading me that "Nanette" was a practical possibility, not just an exciting idea, and she sent me to see Jack Shaw. In no time he not only had a score and libretto for me but had arranged to motor me with his daughters to Brighton to see a matinée on Clarence Pier. We came away blissfully confident that we had seen nothing we could not do better, and by the time we got home it was all tied up and nothing could be easier—so young and eager were the twins and so conceited was I.

Lessons in musical comedy dancing and tap must start at once, so recruiting of dancers was the first step. We began with four girls from the

Red Triangle Club who had worked up a dance routine for their own show there. They got friends to join them. For chorus boys we enlisted four bank juniors and various members of the Terrace Tennis Club. All full of enthusiasm, but none with any stage experience whatsoever.

Jack Shaw was completely sold on the idea, which was just as well, for he was my key man with his interest in the theatre, his dancing daughters and his band. He persuaded his co-directors to let us take the Carlton for a full week—seven performances. Pat Shaw would play "Nanette" and Betty would be Ballet Mistress (or the other way round if I preferred: it really didn't matter!) He and Wilby Shaw would play the two pianos (which the score demanded) in the band. He would give Geoffrey Hewitt all the help he could as accompanist at rehearsals etc. And he would provide the Booking Office.

But there the enthusiasm ended. Welcher let me know in no uncertain terms that this one was not for him. Nicholls did agree to carry on as Business Manager, but sadly and with serious reservations as to the wisdom of the whole idea. I had difficulty in casting the principals and one or two of the chorus gave up after a week or two. Peggy Merrick, whom I had banked on for the sophisticated "Lucille", summoned me to her home to learn, in a scene that would have done credit to a great tragedienne, that she was pregnant. I suddenly seemed to be without any friends at all.

So what! I would produce it myself in addition to playing the comedy lead. I comforted myself with the thought that such a show depends so much on the musical director and the ballet mistress that the producer has little creative work to do. I sorely needed a second comedian and in this I was lucky. Jack Perham, who had been so good as Bunthorne in "Patience", agreed to join me. I was lucky too, in finding at Longburton, a real live genuine Gaiety Girl in Gladys Robinson to play the essentially large and florid "Flora from Nice".

So the dancing and comedy teams were set, except for Pauline, the straight-Jane maid; and to my amazement Doris said she would play the part. Now Doris had never appeared on a stage in her life, nor had she ever shown the least desire to do so, and I am convinced that her only motive now was to back me up in what was going to be a difficult job and could prove a disaster.

It was Doris, too, who suggested that Dulcie Hunt ought to play Lucille in place of Peggy Merrick. This was a risk; Dulcie had been a sweet little Peep-Bo in "Mikado" and had done Props in "Tons of Money"; she had a nice voice, both in singing and in speech, but she was too young for the part and, I thought, lacked the necessary authority. But Doris, as so often, had judged well and Dulcie went on to henpeck Perham and charm everyone else.

We needed to strengthen the chorus voices and the score provided for this by separating the "maids" (dancers) from the "marrieds" (singers). We separated the men in the same way but called them all "bachelors". Thus, in came some of the Operatic Society folk. Redvers Courage and his wife, Mrs. Morris, Ethel Young, Edna Russell and others, including the first of the Dyke family to join the Players, Tom.

Finally, came Cicely Avery to play Sue Smith (my wife). She had recently come to Sherborne on her husband's appointment as Headmaster of Abbey School. Cicely was to play an important role in our early productions and when a few years later she died at a tragically early age, we lost a great friend.

So, when finally cast I found that only George and John Elliott and Dulcie Hunt had come on with me from the "Tons of Money" company into our second production. Moreover, of ten principals, four had never appeared on the stage in their lives, nor had 70% of the chorus; the musical director was an unknown quantity and I was pretty depressed about my own efforts to learn tap-dancing! I practised hard every day on the stone floor of the scullery to the annoyance of the family, but I never became very good. Not so the "maids and the bachelors" whose progress, with verve and enthusiasm, really kept my faith in the show alive. Betty danced with them in the line and won their complete confidence and loyalty. Hers was a tremendous achievement, and she was only just sixteen.

Staging was not difficult. Unlike most of the musicals of the day, "Nanette" had only three sets, though one was a big exterior with a rostrum, steps and an upstairs widow entrance, which did not stack easily. Again we hired from Carlton Fredericks for only £19, including carriage! Costumes were conventional and simple to arrange amongst ouselves though the grls designed and made a smart little ensemble dress for their opening numbers. Again, we paid all our own personal expenses.

Advance bookings were poor. Mr. Nicholls' doubts were shared, not only by others of his committee, but, it seemed, by the whole town. Our list of Patrons was much shorter this time and whereas last year we had succeeded in making it the thing to do to come to the play, this time the tea-table talk took on condescending, even disparaging tones. I came in for considerable criticism personally: it was madness to think we could fill the Carlton for a whole week—nobody ever had: how could amateurs, and youngsters at that, hope to put across a modern musical? Who was this Geoffrey Hewitt, the Conductor? Alcock had let success go to his head and had badly overreached himself. It was a worry, for I knew all too well they could be right.

We had one new and very good friend, however. At that time, and for a very brief period, Sherborne had its own weekly newspaper, "The Sherborne Post". They made a point of printing many pictures and gave us a splendid spread of photographs taken at rehearsal at the Woolmington Hall, with a flattering write-up of what they saw. It must have helped.

The rehearsals themselves went confidently forward. Betty, Geoffrey and I worked happily together, and the young company worked hard and with great enjoyment. Perham and I combined well as a comedy team and though we were still weak in voices, some of the dancing was going better than I would have thought possible. But the bookings were still poor. We felt sure we had a good show but nobody seemed to believe us and it looked certain that we would make a loss, for expenses had risen despite our efforts. Worse, we had no funds at all, having given away every penny of the "Tons of Money" takings.

The two grand pianos were moved into the orchestra pit on the Saturday afternoon and that evening's cinema audiences were treated to a special interlude of selections from "Nanette" played by Jack and Wilby Shaw during which publicity slides were shown on the screen. We hoped it would help the "Popular Night" on Monday—seats 9d—2/6d. It did too; Monday was well sold and the end of the week booking was fair, but the remainder, alas was dreadfully thin. It was very worrying.

I remember the Sunday "get-in" as a day in which every available minute was used to the best purpose but still left no time for an adequate dress rehearsal. Alan Seager, one of the Carlton proprietors, had assumed responsibility for "back stage" and it was considered politic to call him Stage Manager, but it was John Elliott, as "Property Master" who quietly provided the knowledge and experience, and he had a tough job. There was much delay in dismantling the new cinema screen and stowing it safely; the three sets of scenery were cumbersome and difficult to stack allowing space for chorus entries. We were still setting long after the Band Call.

I thought Geoffrey's orchestra rehearsal would never end, but his persistence was fully justified and well rewarded. The Overture and two Entr'actes are integral and important items in "Nanette"; the instrumental combination, built around the two pianos, is unusual and the players were new to each other. They were nine strings, two saxophones, two trumpets, trombone and percussion—seventeen in all, and by the time Geoffrey was through we had an exciting introduction to each act. But it left us time only to rehearse the musical numbers, scene changes and spotlight cues.

So our young and inexperienced company faced the first night of a new and challenging type of show without the benefit of a complete run-through and with the prospect of a near-empty second night tomorrow. Mindful of Dr. Jack's words last year, I had saved a week of my annual holiday for the show with the idea of reducing the strain, but I am sure I should have been better off at work, for I got myself into a dreadful state of nerves. It seemed certain that all the doubts and misgivings of friends would be justified and that all the more caustic prophets would greatly enjoy themselves. It had been crazy to take such absurd risks, not only with the reputation so far built up, but in spending so much when we had absolutely no reserves at all. By the time doors opened I was wishing with all my heart that I had never thought of Amateur Players of Sherborne, marvelling that I had ever pretended to be a comedian, and hoping the Carlton would catch fire or something.

But we were in for some wonderful surprises. First we, and the doubters, had reckoned without the strength of the Show itself. The fact is, "Nanette" cannot fail. She has been kicked around now for nearly fifty years during which she has had some terrible mauling to my knowledge, but she always attracts an audience and always sends them home happy.

As "The Belle of New York" had done thirty years earlier, "Nanette" led a fashion. She was to the twenties what "Oklahoma" would be to the forties and "My Fair Lady" to the fifties. Strangely, when the show opened at the Palace Theatre, London, where its first run of 665 performances began on 11th March 1925, it had not yet played in New York, although an American company had acted it in Chicago for some months—(without "I want to be Happy"!) It was the London production which made it the most famous musical play of its time in the world.

Our first surprise came with the reception accorded the overture. It was presented in show-band style, with F.O.H. Spotlights from the projection box sweeping down on Jack and Wilby Shaw as they led into the first hint of "Tea for Two". From behind the curtain, we could sense the air of excitement and anticipation as the tunes first made famous ten years earlier had feet tapping right through the audience. The applause at the end thrilled us all. As someone said later, "You had a winner before the curtain went up".

Our performance was, I believe, tense, over-stressed and edgy, but it was wonderfully received. The comedy that had died on us weeks ago suddenly regained all its spontaneity, the dances their verve and snap, the melodies a freshness we had forgotten. All in response to an audience who seemed to be willing us on to success, whose laughter and applause brought them right into the show with us.

We had built three specialities into the musical items: they all went better than we had thought possible and all were the subject of comment next day. The first, intended only as a short encore to "You can dance with any girl", was a tap dance by three of the "bachelors"—Bob Hazzard, Ross Biles and Joey Brown. In teaching them, Betty had kept to the simplest of basic steps and had concentrated on drill, and the result looked astonishingly accomplished. The three boys had worked tremendously hard for weeks and weeks and deserved every bit of the great reception they won. Applause broke out well before the end of their act and with their effective exit they really did stop the show, the audience refusing to let them go. It was at this moment, and not before, that I felt that we must have won through.

Early in the third act Pat (Nanette) performed "Table Top Toe Tap", a dance which won her much admiration. John Elliott had made what looked like a small decorative occasional table, but was, in fact, a robust stand firmly fixed to the stage. It had a plate glass top and housed hidden coloured lights shining upwards, which provided the only illumination as Pat tapped out a neat little rhythm on her points. It was difficult and dangerous, for there must have been the possibility that she would miss the edge, but it looked sensational from the front.

Finally, as part of the "Take a Litle One-Step" number came the Mirror Dance. The men's chorus hauled on a large gilt mirror and in which Nanette could be seen pirouetting and dancing with her own image. In this the twins did succeed in actually deceiving many of the audience and the burst of applause as Betty stepped out of the mirror to join her sister was quite something. The Mirror Dance was indeed a "talking point" next day.

(Both this and the "Table Top Toe Tap" had been Jack Shaw's ideas and the twins continued to perform them for years.)

And so to the hectic Finale. As we belted out "Happy" for the last time, applause broke out and grew and grew well before the Curtain into what must be remembered as one of the most generous ovations of my experience. And never was one more needed, or more welcome when it came.

As we took curtain after curtain I ought to have felt a sense of triumph, but no. Relief certainly and gratitude, overflowing gratitude to a generous and forgiving audience, but I simply could not join in the congratulations and back-slapping. Too much had gone wrong or fallen short. Too many ragged chorus entries and bunched exits caused, like the too long intervals, by bad scenery packing—something to be seen to next morning—if we could somehow avoid Alan Seager. Then I was unhappy about the performance, feeling that we had just scrambled through. All the energy and high spirits had smacked of desperation, and, in this I had been the worst culprit, obviously striving for effect, over-stressing and mistiming. How much of all this had crossed the footlights I could not know, and anyhow that was not the point. We had to get it right.

Over all loomed the black cloud of financial worry. The wretched booking plans haunted me. By any reckoning it was a very dejected and anxious comedian who went home to bed. For him the "Nanette" opening has remained ever since the most hazardous and exhausting first night of them all.

Only when Doris brought me up a hot drink to bed did I find something comforting and heart-warming to remember about the show — her own simple direct little performance. She had carried the responsibility of opening the first scene without any fuss, won the first laugh for us, and by the time she appeared in her Edwardian bathing costume all hearts were with her. She appeared completely unaware of her success and was concerned only for me.

Almost reluctantly my spirits rose a little next day. I found Shaws busy booking, mostly for later in the week, and Jack told me the phone "had not stopped ringing all the morning". Comment on the opening performance was flattering. Yet I remained anxious. I believe I have never been able to relish or revel in success. I get excited and elated at the prospect of it, but once achieved, no, the satisfaction of success is not for me and this time I did not even recognise it.

Not until the evening. Then, and it will never be forgotten, walking down from Bristol Road with Doris, carrying the case of clothes she had pressed for me, I turned from Greenhill into Newland, and there they were —a queue stretching the length of the road. The sight brought a great lump to my throat. People, hundreds of them, were queuing to see us. The show had sold itself. We were home.

We played to capacity for the remainder of the week, including the matinée—(this last so pleased us that Reg Chaffin came to photograph the entrance to the Carlton with our "House Full" board in position). Trouble between the theatre proprietors and Superintendent Cherrett about the permitted standing room was music to us. On Wednesday out came the "Sherborne Post" with most extravagant praise. This, with The Western Gazette's more sober and more valued review on Thursday and the fact that people were being turned away led to a suggestion from the Carlton that we should run part of a second week, but it was not practicable and, in any case, we simply could not have stood the physical strain.

The Western Gazette paid us the compliment of coming again on the last night to report the closing speeches, the presentation of £51 to the Town Nurse Fund and the news that 3500/4000 people had seen "Nanette".

No production has ever bitten so deeply into me. I expect many of us have a recurring dream, one that crops up over and over again. Well, mine is always of "Nanette". We get a music cue for a number, only to realise we have not even touched it, or we face the show tomorrow and have not yet rehearsed Act III. Time and time again through the years I have awakened in a sweat over it.

But it is not always a nightmare—some of the best moments come back too and I am glad of that, for the show was an important milestone in my life. It established Amateur Players of Sherborne on an undeniably firm footing and it marked the end of my career as a comic. I was thirty, and for twenty years, from my school "dormy" shows at the age of ten, my strongest asset had been the ability to "make 'em laugh". It had enabled me to make my mark and it had earned me good money when it was much needed. "Nanette", according to reports, had proved a great vehicle for me, and it is good to look back and feel that, as a comedian, I had finished on the top note.

"Nanette" got by on its high spirits, its tunes and its comedy. Yet in my memory the big moment of the show was silent, and it belonged to Dulcie Hunt. Her "Hubby Gone Blues" song in Act III was in complete contrast to all else in the score: and as she finished, alone, upstage (the supporting "bachelors" having withdrawn), she stood quite still, immensely appealing, her last sad note true and sustained. Then; then came a long, long silence before the applause broke—the silence of an audience held rapt. It was a moment professionals strive for. It is rarely achieved by an amateur and Dulcie won it night after night.

This may, of course, have had nothing to do with my coming change of direction, but the fact remains that quite suddenly I came to realise that there was more to it than making them laugh. I wanted to be able to grip an audience in silence. What's more, I thought I knew how I would like to try. I had been lent a copy of "Night Must Fall" (Emlyn Williams). The play was still running at the Duchess.

CHAPTER NINE

PAUSE

Although 1936 was to be a significant year in the development of A.P.S., several factors combined to prevent an immediate successor to "Nanette". There was, predictably, some pressure for another musical and I had considered both "Mercenary Mary" and "Mr. Cinders", liking the tunes and hating the "book" in each case. Any such possibility, however, was ruled out by the news of the intended revival of Sherborne Operatic Society and clearly, they had priority.

Next, I received a flattering offer to produce "Nanette" all over again for Glastonbury Operatic Society at a professional fee much too good to refuse. All the same, I would probably have turned it down had I not learnt just then that "Night Must Fall", on which I had set my heart, would not be released until the following year.

The resuscitated society staged "The Gondoliers" at the Carlton with Cicely's husband, H. W. Avery as the new musical director and Mrs. Maddison, from Dorchester, producing. The two gondoliers were played by two parsons, Gerald Ellison (now the Bishop of London) and D. B. Eperson, then I believe, the School Chaplain. Peggy Merrick and Cicely Avery were their two counterparts and Casilda was sweetly sung by a newcomer who was later to become a valued member of A.P.S., Margaret King. The opera went sufficiently well to warrant one more effort, "The Quaker Girl", but that was, indeed, the end.

Meanwhile, off I went to Glastonbury, with Pat and Betty Shaw to teach the dancing and their father to provide the transport and, on occasion, deputise as pianist.

It was quite an experience to work as a paid professional. Pleasant to produce the show free from money worries and responsibilities, but hateful feeling under an obligation to the committee who employed me. The show went well—"Nanette" cannot fail—but I declined the offer to return for "Les Cloches de Cornville" the following year.

The only way in which this adventure touches upon our story is the sorry fact that its timing left me insufficient weeks to study and I failed my Accountancy examination. So there was to be yet another year with no Spring production. My failure could not, however, be blamed entirely on the Glastonbury work, for this was a time of awakening to a fervent and serious interest in the theory of play production and presentation. All too frequently the book on "The Practice and Law of Banking" was put down in favour of "The Technique of Play Production". For the first time I was coming to realise how much more there is to the theatre than just the craft of entertaining, though this remains for me the absolute criterion for anything theatrical. For the first time I was becoming aware of the Author and the significance of true interpretation. And the more I read, the more I realized how much there was to learn and the more deeply I became involved. Movement, Grouping, Triangulation, Orchestration of Dialogue, Stress, Attack, Pause, Business, Period, Manners: the principles of Decor, Costume (about which I still know nothing), Lighting, Effects. So much to grasp it scared me. Yet it was comforting to find that some, at least, of the truth of what I was reading had already been absorbed by instinct and experience. Now I was discovering the reasons behind it all. (No wonder banking got neglected!) But I needed practice, and a happy coincidence was to provide it in the right place at the right time.

Sherborne now had a new Vicar. The Rev. W. M. Askwith was keenly interested in young people and their welfare, and to this end great improvements were being made at the Church Hall. The old gallery was converted into a clubroom (except for two rows which still remain), the stage was given a proscenium (which however did not go up to the ceiling, so that stage lighting spilled into the auditorium), and furnished with nice blue tableau curtains. It still did not extend from wall to wall, but it was far more practical than in the days of "The Ghost Train".

Here I was asked to produce "Eliza Comes to Stay" for the newly formed Young Communicants' Fellowship. Gerald Ellison played the juvenile lead, which guaranteed keen competition for the name-part, and Maurie Welcher provided the lighting. The Vicar, keen to interest as many young people as possible and realising that many, especially boys, would not want to appear on the stage, mustered the young carpenters, painters, electricians and handymen into quite an impressive back-stage team.

And that is the significant aspect of "Eliza" for the future of A.P.S. For in them I found the nucleus of the Players' first Black Gang, those who, during some of the years ahead, were to become almost our elite, responsible for mounting the big "Scarlet Pimpernel", taking us to Yeovil, Taunton and Bristol for B.D.L. Festivals, seeing us in and out of every village hall and school for miles around Sherborne with our war-time shows, touring our plays after the war and staging us twice at Theatre Royal, Bristol. Much of our story could not be told but for our Black Gang, and the originals came from "Eliza".

It was a delightfully happy and carefree little show, enjoying good support from many quarters. It was good exercise for me in my new role of drama producer and, happy to be back in "fit-up" again, I was full of ideas for what could be done at the Church Hall, if and when . . .

But not yet. First, back to the Carlton.

CHAPTER TEN

CHANGE OF COURSE

Alf, Captain A. T. Collings, R.A. commissioned on the field during the 1914-18 War, was the landlord of the Mermaid Hotel, in Bristol Road. Easy-going, generous and big-hearted, he was, unsurprisingly closely concerned in the British Legion, Sherborne Benevolent Fund.

The Mermaid was my "Local", indeed it was the Lloyds Bank local, most of our staff living nearby, and Alf held a special place amongst our customers. (In those days Bank staff everywhere used to see the New Year in at the office coping with the half-yearly balance work, and for years we kept up a custom of telephoning Alf and Mrs. Collings at midnight with New Year Greetings.) Peter Caines, our Chief Clerk was Treasurer of the local British Legion Branch, so when he, George Merrick and I were all at the Mermaid one evening it came about quite naturally and fittingly that a decision was made to "do a play" for the Benevolent Fund. Alf at once offered his club-room to us for rehearsals free of charge. We declined such open-handed generosity, but the rent we did pay him was little more than sufficient to cover his outgoings.

Thus it was that the Mermaid became the Players' first home and remained so until after Alf's death ten years later. There was nothing he and his wife would not do to make us comfortable and welcome. Except for a weekly R.A.O.B. Lodge night, we had the run of the club-room for all rehearsals, conferences and social get-togethers, and the fact that we now had a base did much towards our establishment as a permanent body. In any Roll of "Friends of the Players" Alf and Mrs. Collings would take an honoured place amongst the earliest.

There was no difficulty in choosing the play. "Night Must Fall" could not have become available at a better time. Its author's name had become famous amongst the new men of the theatre, its title alone made an impact. The play was the first of the psychological thrillers. A murder play without mystery, it was not concerned with melodramatic situation. Instead, Elmyn Williams took us inside the criminal's mind, the story moving forward with a chilling inevitability. No new play of the period was more widely discussed. It broke all previous records at the Duchess before transferring to the Cambridge Theatre. As a local attraction "Night Must Fall" was just the right play to appeal to the greater number of men who might be expected to support a British Legion show.

To me, this great piece of theatre provided the ideal vehicle for giving effect to the lessons on production I was trying so hard to absorb. Doubtless many of my ideas and theories were mistaken, but out of all the reading, exercise and experiment there emerged a fairly clear conception of a producer's function. And with it came an urge amounting almost to an obsession. To me there became no more exciting or desirable project than to bring a play alive, from the detailed study of the work, sensing the author's intention, breathing life into the dialogue, placing the action, developing the illusion of reality: and then to present to an expectant audience, willing to "suspend their disbelief", the memorable experience that a play should be. I soon learnt that the eventual performance never matches up to one's first vision of the play, but I have always believed it will do so next time!

As a producer then, I came to see myself as part interpreter, part illusionist, but not at all as an organiser.

Creating an illusion acceptable to an audience, however willing to believe, clearly involves more than interpretation of character. It also demands the producer's imagination and ingenuity in building the stage picture, its decor, lighting, costume, effects. In this I was fortunate in having some elementary knowledge gained in a variety of ways from school and early concert party days right through to "Nanette", and I knew enough of the practical aspects of presentation to talk the right language to stage carpenters, stage managers, electricians and others selected more for their technical ability in specialised fields than for their stagecraft.

As to interpretation, I was convinced from the start that the one essential quality of any production is unity. There can only be one interpretation of the author's meaning and intention. One idea, right or wrong, of the characters, the atmosphere, the emphasis, the "convention". This insistence on "one idea only" was to get me into difficulties on only rare occasions. Usually actors and stage staff alike, particularly the latter, are quite ready to accept and carry through the producer's interpretation provided his views are definite and clearly defined. I have never managed to rid myself of that first sense of awe at the weight of responsibility resting upon a producer and it still amazes me to see how, in some amateur societies, the task is tossed light-heartedly from one player to another in turn without realising he can be little better than an organiser. What hope can there be for the standard of an orchestra if the conductor's baton is handed casually from player to player?

These then were the lines—and they can certainly be faulted—upon which our productions were to be run, starting with "Night Must Fall". In the quest for unity, for "one idea only" I had no qualms about playing Dan myself as well as undertaking the production of the play, with Maurice to hold the book for me when required. Nor was there any hesitation as to the actress for Dora, the unfortunate little maid-of-all-work who had been seduced by Dan. Doris was adamant that if anyone was to be seen to be in the family way by me it was going to be her! And, bless her, she did us proud, with a simple direct little portrayal of incoherent suffering that was infinitely appealing.

Casting proved easy—with one great stroke of luck. From our previous shows came W. J. Cordy (an impressive Lord Chief Justice), Cicely Avery (playing throughout in a wheel-chair), Welcher (acting this time), Tom Dyke and Peggy Merrick, who had decided she was right for Olivia, the important part that had been created by Angela Baddeley. Eva Gillam, the Fairy Queen in "Iolanthe" joined us to play the "heavy" and Welcher introduced a new young mistress at Lord Digby's School, Winifred Hickson to play a small part as a District Nurse.

I have never since had a production so fully prepared before rehearsal as "Night Must Fall". Not only did I know my own part; I had made detailed sketches of all the others, plotted all the moves and marked for stress, climax etc. I had been to London and had come back with notes on the original music and the press-cuts from theatre bill-boards, obtained from the Duchess Theatre, where a man in a little room miles up above the stage had been wonderfully kind and helpful. And I had seen Walter Peacock, then Mr. Williams' agent who had told me we would be the first amateur production of "Night Must Fall" in the South of England. (We were to have been the first in the Country, but the author had permitted a Welsh company to beat the gun and then another in the North pipped us by a week.)

If I approached our first rehearsal at the Mermaid well prepared, I had also worked myself up into a great state of tension—this play meant a very great deal to me. It was disconcerting therefore to be greeted with a message that Mrs. Merrick was visiting friends in Weymouth and would arrive late or not at all. I managed to trace and telephone the Weymouth address and told a surprised and rather hurt Peggy that she need never come to a rehearsal again. We were not very good friends for some time after that.

So my carefully prepared first rehearsal started with a somewhat ruffled producer and no female lead. Miss Hickson was asked to read Olivia. She took over the part, and in the event acted the rest of us off the stage. This chance casting was a stroke of great good fortune. John Elliott's newly arrived wife, Winnie joined us to play the nurse.

"Night Must Fall" is remembered as perhaps the smoothest, easiest, most harmonious production of them all. Mr. Meredith Thomas and Gen. R. L. Waller joined us in committee to represent the British Legion interests and they had no very onerous task in gaining support for the show, for it sold easily.

Publicity work brought into the Players one, who for many years, proved a staunch friend who has left his own memorial in the shape of the A.P.S. crest. Mervyn Davies was a colleague of mine at Lloyds Bank, and like me may, perhaps, (or perhaps not—you never know), have missed his vocation, for he was—is, a good artist and a brilliant cartoonist. For "Night Must Fall" he executed a large, horrific cut-out of me as the murderous pageboy which stood impressively in the foyer of the Carlton.

We got a splendid free-boost also from the "News Chronicle" which featured us as number 57 in their series on "Western Footlights". This so pleased us that it was reprinted in our programme. Headed **"Sherborne's Successful Amateurs"** it continued:—

'Originality is the keynote of Amateur Players of Sherborne. Strictly they are a band of independent enthusiasts working under the general direction of Mr. Fred. B. Alcock for the benefit of local charities. If financial results are any criterion, Amateur Players of Sherborne must surely have found the recipe for success. Their production of "Tons of Money" two years ago resulted in £100 for the Yeatman Hospital, while the following year, "No, No, Nanette" made £51 for the local Nursing Association. Such results are achieved by the drastic reduction of expenses to the minimum consistent with efficiency, the sacrifices of the company in bearing their own expenses, the handing over without reserve of every penny made and—the support of the public of Sherborne and district,' . . .

and so on, with a good picture of me as Dan in "Night Must Fall". This, together with our plug of "The First Amateur Production in the South of England" attracted interest over a wide area.

Hugh Sawtell's programme itself was quite a production. Sixteen pages inside the two-colour cover gave a Foreword about the Sherborne Benevolent Fund of the British Legion over the signature of G. O'Hanlon, President and H. J. Hatton, Secretary; a page about the Players with acknowledgements and another, "Introducing 'Night Must Fall' " about Emlyn Williams, noting that he had already written, inter alia, "Spring 1600".

The names of some of our generous advertisers come now as happy reminders of Sherborne in 1937. Harden Trevett & Son, "the old Sherborne Ironmongers are still at the old address". Sticklands, "Night Must Fall, so sleep in our cosy pyjamas"; Soyers, "Best products from the sea—phone early for luncheon delivery"; Carter and Company, E. J. Upsall, Walter Bown and Son, The Dorsetshire Brewery Co., Hill & Boll Ltd., D.C. Eectric, E. C. Burden . . . But they have not all gone: The Three Wishes, Freemans "for All Sports", Seymours, Phillips and Son, Mould & Edwards, and others. All friends of the Players, backing our efforts by enabling us to give away every penny paid for programmes. P. J. Shaw, "Music Salon, Sherborne" advertised in his own way, by providing us with our first use of canned music to show off his newest developments in gramophone reproduction. A full page in the programme listed the music for each interval.

Nor was this our only electrical aid. The play, like many others, divided the Acts into several scenes, when the house would remain darkened and programmes could not be consulted. So Jim Cowan and Reg Dicker, two of my Young Communicants' Black Gang, made a large illuminated calendar which stood at the side of the proscenium and at the appropriate time announced for all to see, "Twelve Days Later" or "Half an Hour Later". Apart from its novelty the calendar proved a great asset and was used in several of our later productions.

"Before The Play" (not "Prologue"—author), "The Court of Criminal Appeal" was played in pin spots only. We put W. J. Cordy up on a very high rostrum so that he would be looking down on an audience as he delivered judgement. (And very imposing he looked. So impressive indeed that I was half afraid to tell him he was inaudible at the dress rehearsal—but I managed it!)

Crouching unseen at his feet was a scene-shifter, hiding there so that the rostrum could be removed with the actor and the lights brought up on the main set to a music cue timed at nine seconds. He was a lad of 16 who was to become our most illustrious stage-hand. Fifteen years later I was greatly honoured to be his guest at the re-opening of London's Old Vic Theatre in Waterloo Road when, as Michael Innes, he was Stage Manager there, having graduated via Bristol Old Vic School and Bristol Old Vic Company of which he was for a time Stage Director. To us he was and still is "Bunter" Fudge, son of Ted Fudge, saddler of South Street and an early childhood friend of Joy. Bunter was to play an increasingly important role in our progress over the next ten years, but not the least of his successes was the nine-second change in "Night Must Fall". Nine seconds during which the spots dimmed on the Lord Chief Justice, Holst's "The Perfect Fool" merged into the sound of distant church bells and the lights came up on Mrs. Bramson's bungalow.

We gave only three performances of "Night Must Fall", having decided against a matinée because the play was considered unsuitable for children—a sign of the times. Maurice Welcher, in addition to acting a part, played the harmonium (off), delivered the oil, imitated an owl and was Stage Director. He had held the book for me in final rehearsals and now saw the curtain up. All I had to concern me was my own part and I remember the performance with unclouded pleasure. Absolutely everything went right, or so it seemed to me. Cicely manoeuvred her wheelchair in and out of the doors and around the furniture as if she had lived in it for years. Hickson (funny how she was never Winifred, though to me she was Livvy for years after playing Olivia) succeeded in projecting from a clever portrayal of a flat-heeled, "sensible", repressed spinster, a tremendous depth of emotional tension. Playing our final scene together, with an audience gripped by the play, I believe we did build an atmosphere of suspense which went some way to doing justice to the author. For me it was an experience to remember. For Livvy too, I believe.

As to my on performance, I don't know. One never does. There had been the fear, and I know it was shared by the company, that I might not be accepted seriously, having been known, for what it was worth, only as a comedian. W. S. Gilbert said it: "An accepted wit has but to say 'pass the mustard' and they'll roar their ribs out". So I was nervous, but by the Act I curtain we knew it was alright. The laughs came when we wanted them and so did the silences. The generosity at my final curtain call meant a great deal more to me than perhaps it should, and, small-minded though it may be, it still deighted me when some thirty-five years later on a visit to Sherborne I was greeted in a shop with "But I always remember you as that murdering page-boy". It's a long time for an amateur performance to be remembered.

"Night Must Fall" made £45 of which The British Legion distributed two-thirds to needy local ex-Servicemen and their families as a help at Christmas time, and the remainder was sent to a distressed area in South Wales—a sad reflection on the times we lived in then. Everyone expressed gratitude for something to somebody and everyone was happy—with the exception of the Carlton Theatre proprietors. Deprived of another "Nanette" harvest, they sought with some success to increase their 50% share of the gross takings by charging various extras; and relations, I fear, became a little strained. Clearly, if we were to continue to play at the Carlton and at the same time—our first principle—spare no effort to make the last penny possible for a good cause, some better arrangement would have to be made for the future.

There are two little postscripts to the story of "Night Must Fall" which have a bearing on our future course. First, amongst visiting societies who came to see the play were friends from Taunton (still calling me Ko-Ko), including some of Taunton Thespians. They were then hard at work on "The Scarlet Pimpernel" to be staged in the Spring of 1938 at Taunton Odeon, with Percy Olds and Margaret Way as Sir Percy and Lady Blakeney. Their producer was John Wilkins whom I was to come to regard as one of the most talented and dedicated amateurs I have met. His "Tovarich" at Taunton still lives in my memory as an outstanding achievement in Amateur Theatre. John, for future reference, was also the Hon. Secretary of the British Drama League, Western Area, Central Division.

Second, I neglected to mention earlier that our sixteen page programme contained an advertisement which we had inserted ourselves announcing the Old Fosterians' Dramatic Society in "The Sport of Kings" by Ian Hay at the Carlton Theatre on December 6, 7, 8. This date was a little too near Christmas to suit them.

The Old Fosterians had first taken their annual production to the Carlton in November 1936 with "The Middle Watch", in which Ernest Hulme gave a portrayal of Marine Ogg to be remembered as a gem, surely one of his best, and that says a lot.

In November 1936 there had been no problem, for I was busy in Glastonbury, but obviously there could be some competition for the November date in future unless we could compromise in some way.

CHAPTER ELEVEN

SECOND STAGE

Spring 1938, and only one thought in mind. I simply had to finish with the Institute of Bankers exams. I was thirty-two, already ten years older than many finalists and I still had two tough subjects to pass, of which I had already failed one. Either I would gain my A.I.B. this time, or I would give up and then I would either end my banking career as a second cashier or I would get out of it and try to make a living in the theatre. No, I wouldn't. There were Doris and Joy and Judy and my Mother to be thought of. Besides, I hadn't the talent or the courage. So I would have to pass the exam.

For five months I worked at it as I had never worked before and curiously I began to find it less and less of a chore. At long last I was finding some interest in the theory of my job. As the big week approachd I gained confidence, and the night before I had to take the first subject I was happy to relax and rest. That evening Maurie Welcher looked in for a chat and quietly mentioned that the Carlton had sold our date in the following November to the Old Fosterians for a revival of "The Ghost Train".

I am not proud of my unreasoning, inarticulate fury. I raced down to Alan Seager, at his garage in Coldharbour and there ensued one of the very few really blazing rows of my life. Seager advanced all the sensible arguments. It was, after all, first come first served. They wanted comedy for the box office. The Old Fosterians were a permanent Society whereas there was no knowing whether we even intended to continue or what we would do. The Old Fosterians were not so bound by these ideas of making money, and so less inclined to haggle over terms. On and on it went and as the whisky got lower and lower in the bottle so did my own spirits. The very night before my vital exam; and I was getting drunk. When I awoke next morning with a frightful headache and a frosty wife I had one vivid memory still in mind. I had told the Carlton to go to Hell—for good.

*   *   *   *   *

The exam results came out in July. I had passed, placed No. 320 out of 1426: Not brilliant, but not bad. After six years struggle, I could now put "Cert. A.I.B." after my name, and, suddenly banking had become an interesting occupation. My £30 gratuity bought us a caravan holiday at Maidencombe, and there I worked happily in preparing "The Scarlet Pimpernel" to be presented (by arrangement with Miss Julia Neilson) at the Church Hall, Sherborne on 2nd November.

Things had gone wonderfully well, so much better than I ever deserved following my stupidity over the Carton. Having burnt our boats for us I had left us without a theatre at just the wrong time. The Operatic Society

46

had finally wound up, so there was a demand for a big show wih a large cast and if only I had been sensible we could now have staged one at the Carlton in the Spring. I had lost us the services of Jach Shaw for Box Office and Music and John Elliott as Stage Manager. (He would be with Old Fosterians.) There was no reason to believe we would be allowed to alter the stage at the Church Hall as necessary, or that audiences woud follow us there to sit on wooden chairs. Oh yes, I had made a fool of myself.

Yet it had all come right so easily. First there were "The Others". How good it was to find we were now a company, our problems were problems shared, to be tackled by four or five or six of us over a drink at the Mermaid. No formality, no "procedure". Reprehensible by accepted standards no doubt, but that is as it was. The others all agreed we would stick to our November date and make the best of the Church Hall.

And here we made a new friend in Mr. C. W. H. Steele, who represented the Church Hall Trustees. From the very start he understood our difficulties and our requirements. In turn we had to recognise the multi-purpose use of the Hall. Thus we reached a flexible but effective agreement whereby the formal rent we paid was modest (no troubles over Entertainment Tax here), but from each hiring we did something extra to improve the Hall's amenities. We made a start at once on improving seating. True, our first show in the new home provided only two rows of the (then) new style packing chairs but it was something.

Our first task was to make the stage practicable. It had to be extended to the walls by substantial, but removable, platforms; the proscenium had to be built up to the roof and the fixed surround-curtain supports replaced by roof-timbers to carry pulleys and lines. That done, we would have the one vital property of any stage—space. Space on either side and, just as important, above (one day we would fly the front tabs—a curtain, when used, should rise and descend, not come apart in the middle—but that would not be for a long time yet). We could afford to do only the bare essentials and by the cheapest possible means. Even so, Minterne's bill for £60 set us a problem, for we had no money at all. Peter Caines, George Merrick and I therefore screwed up courage to ask our Manager, Mr. Gobey if the Players account (Balance Nil) could overdraw for a few weeks. Mr. Gobey made very heavy weather of it, but agreed in the end. In the event we need not have troubled him because we worked out and launched a new Subscribers Scheme to replace the Patrons and, such was the goodwill we were now enjoying, we soon had funds in hand—even before our show was advertised. Things had gone well indeed.

We owed "The Scarlet Pimpernel" to George Philpott (A. H. Philpott and Son, Grocers, Trendle Street). George had been one of the "Nanette" boys and was to be a valued member of our black gang for some years. Indeed, he had much to do with forming the gang and it all came about through his friendship with David Smith, stage carpenter of Taunton Thespians. He was wildly enthusiastic about their show, its staging, its crowded houses; and as he talked (while paying-in at the Bank) it began to dawn on me that here we might have a winner for our new "theatre". The required large cast, a "family" show to follow "Night Must Fall", a well-known title, spectacular staging to demonstrate what could be done at the Church Hall . . . And I had good friends in Taunton. It was a possibility.

So it came about that one summery Saturday afternoon, after a few of us had talked it over, Livvy (Hickson) motored me over to Taunton with only the title of our next play in mind. We returned with the Thespians' blessing, John Wilkins' prompt book, the block by Len Mieux for the programme cover and the loan of three big sets of eighteen-foot flats built for The Odeon—the other two were too large even allowing for our big ideas. Yes, we had friends in Taunton.

There was plenty to work on at Maidencombe. The play demanded five full sets, including two exteriors and one to provide a loft, ground floor and cellar (for which we were allowed to cut the trap in the stage floor). There was a cast of forty-one actors (some doubled) and a horse and cart!

Enter Kenneth R. Blackmore, to head a short procession of newcomers who were so to influence the future of the Players as to make "The Pimpernel" a significant milestone in our history. Ken was Bunter's immediate boss at Sherborne R.D.C.—hence the introduction. He had been with the Operatic Society during its brief revival; he was an able handyman, a good organiser, and a super-optimist who believed firmly that nothing was impossible. Just the man to stage-manage this one.

We were generously allowed the use of the Rawson Hall to build, paint and assemble our scenery and here with Bunter Fudge and George Philpott as his lieutenants, Ken cheerfully set about the enormous task of mounting the most cumbersome production we have ever undertaken. For his team we went straight to the Y.C.F. "Eliza" company and they came with youthful enthusiasm—Stanley Axe, Bill Eveleigh, Brian Jones, Austin Mead, Douglas Morgan, George Park, Reg White—our first "Black Gang".

The Taunton "West Barricade", "Fisherman's Rest" and "Lion d'Or" sets, all beautifully done by Len Mieux, had to be matched by our own "Foreign Office Ballroom" and "Sir Percy Blakeney's Garden" and we certainly did our best. Mervyn Davies undertook the decor of the ballroom and Mrs. Gervis and Miss Wickham, two well-known local artists, agreed to paint the garden scene. So many folk seemed ready to help us; Jim Park (Builder, Westbury and I believe Chairman of the Council) made a ramp for the horse to get through the stage-door and a cart with detachable wheels which could be assembled in the wings, otherwise it would not go through the door. The Hon. Mrs. Barnes lent us her very valuable spinet, The Rev. Mother of St. Antonys lent us a grand piano, Mr. Sandford-Wills lent us his massive carved garden seat from The Priory. Such goodwill from everyone: and all I believe because we were now known to be trying earnestly to do more than just amuse ourselves and others.

We did not lose John Elliott after all. He undertook the furnishing and found us some very fine period pieces for the "Fisherman's Rest" and the "Foreign Office Ballroom". Mr. Webb (Grocer, Cheap Street) took over the Box Office and Horace Hamblin joined us to provide "electrical reproduction". (I had known Horace since my earliest days in Sherborne. He was a fine technician and had made the first moving-coil loudspeaker in the district—it filled a whole doorway in his cottage in Newland. I used to sit and marvel at it.)

The obvious problem of accommodation back-stage was solved for us by the offer of space in the Red Triangle Club and a simple awning between the two buildings thus led us to a good scene-dock, furniture store and greenroom, with refreshments. It was all coming so easily now.

"The fewer the props the better the play." By this measure "The Pimpernel" is a thoroughly bad one, for the property plot would daunt any but a very stout heart. But, enter Margery Hall, Director and Secretary of a fine family business, William Seymour & Co., Wine and Spirits Merchants and Mineral Water Manufacturers. As one might expect by now, Margery got let in for the onerous task of props. when paying in at the Bank, but little then did I know with a vital role this new Player was to take in our story. Nor, I suspect, did Marge realise what the Players would do for hers. But that was for the future: for now, yes, she would find the props, over two hundred of them; everything from clay pipes to silver candle snuffers. With two assistants she completed the job exactly as expected—with brisk efficiency.

With one exception, casting was sheer joy, for the response was heart-warming indeed. Everyone it seemed wanted to lend a hand, even if it was only to walk on. From the Operatic Society came Eva Gillam, Redvers and Mrs. Courage, Terry Rudd, Douglas Stewart, Ethel Young amongst others, some from "Eliza" and nearly all the earlier Players. Even the horse was easily cast, for Nancy Young brought us her wonderful little pony. He was, I believe, more than twenty years old and had once been with a circus. He behaved impeccably and we owed a great debt to Nancy Young for the quiet, unfussed way in which she and her pony arrived exactly on time each night, completed their "act" and departed just as neatly.

Jack Perham, my mate from "Nanette" played Sir Percy, Maurie Welcher was the villainous Chauvelin, looking alternately sinister and unhappy—not difficult, bless him—and the other parts fell easily into place, except one. I could not find a Lady Blakeney. Tall, lovely, elegant, aristocratic in bearing, musical voice. We sought her here, we sought her there, we thought we had sought her everywhere. And then she appeared as if by magic, from Yeovil in the person of Helen Palmer who had everything we asked and was talented too. It was a delight to direct her—no temperament, so receptive—and she went on to take the acting honours with all the grace of a true leading lady.

Enter F. W. Forrest, pushed gently by his wife, Blanche who came too. Fred had recently come to Sherborne as Customs and Excise Officer. Elderly, very quiet and unassuming, he accepted the small part of Mr. Hampseed, and I soon realised that we had gained a very fine character actor. His wife was less talented but equally enthusiastic and loyal to the Players. It was their boast in later years that every piece of furniture in their home, except the bed, had appeared in a Players production at some time or other. Good, good friends.

Enter a lively young man to play Armand St. Just. He had a prematurely bald head, a slight limp, a great sense of humour and a gift for mime. Tom Dyke had brought along his young brother Bewsey. Today, still an active member, Bewsey Dyke holds a unique and unassailable position with the Players. No other man has given an unbroken thirty-eight years of service; no other man has produced so many plays for them, eighteen in succession; no other man did more than he to steer the players on to their present successful course. He was to make his first real mark with us in the war-time shows which allowed scope for his gift of impromptu comedy. In the part of Armand St. Just, however, he was less effective, and if truth must be told he was a bit trying at rehearsal at first because he would play the fool, albeit not for long. The fact that we were not there just for fun was soon comprehended and although Bewsey's performance as Armand was unremarkable, his contribution to the production did not end there, for he was the first of the new small-part actors to take off his jacket, join the gang spontaneously and help shift scenery. He was also our self-appointed Stable Lad, armed with bucket and shovel which he kept both before and, more especially, after use in the "cellar" beneath the "Lion D'Or", at the foot of the steps down which poor Chauvelin would be thrust at sword point and the trap slammed shut above him to end the play.

Baroness Orczy's famous novel was first adapted as a play in a scenario by Courtenay Thorpe and received its premiere at the Theatre Royal, Nottingham in 1903. Much was re-written and Scene I added by Fred Terry and Louis Calvert for its first London production at the New Theatre on 5th January 1905. Press notices were poor but the play ran for 1,000 performances in London and then continued to keep Fred Terry and Julia Neilson in almost unbroken employment for many years, playing over 2,000 performances in the provinces and overseas, until shortly before the death of Terry in 1933.

The play was never published, so all our actors had to work on were type-written sheets of their own "lines", and we had to build the framework from the very ground. In this, John Wilkins' prompt-book was a Godsend to me and I doubt whether, in my inexperience, I could have coped at all without it. Even so, many problems beset us in trying to interpret a play which, for all the popularity of the name and the success of the novel, had been no more than a poorly constructed vehicle for old-style actors of "ham". Coming after the easy-flowing natural dialogue from the pen of Emlyn Williams, these hopelessly stilted "speeches", the forced humour, the contrived entrances and exits presented a daunting task. Strange that when we were overcoming the problems of staging so successfully we should be so nonplussed when it came to acting the play.

It proved a valuable and rewarding exercise, one that was to have a lasting effect upon our style of acting for years ahead. During the late twenties and early thirties the English theatre had passed through a ghastly era of "Naturalistic" acting, arising perhaps from misunderstanding the teachings of Komisarjevsky and Stanislavsky, or it may have been the sway of film acting with its need for subtlety and intimacy. Whatever the reason, it was for a time forgotten that stage-acting must be larger than life. The unforgivable sin was "overacting". It was only a passing phase but its overhang unfortunately had a bad and lasting effect on the amateur stage because it gave an apparent authority for the amateur's greatest weakness, that of underplaying in his endeavours to appear "natural".

Perhaps it was my upbringing as an audience-conscious entertainer that jibbed or just the exhibitionist in me, or the seed sown by Frank Benson and Henry Baynton at thet Old Bath Theatre Royal, but the conviction grew in me that we were wrong. I held that if a great professional actor were to appear incognito in an amateur production he would be accused of overacting. And I had some justification, for the voices of the great were being heard against the doctrines of naturalism. Noel Coward—"All acting worth the name is ham." Marie Tempest—"Cover up the 'ham' but don't take it away", Tyrone Guthrie, whose particular abominations were country house comedies, was calling for a larger element of "ham" in acting as opposed to the restraints and repressions of underplaying. Soon the Method School was to arrive to restore the "heart" to acting and amateurs could take courage from observing it in the professional theatre, but in the late thirties one had to be "true to life", never be "stagey" nor play for effect. It was deadly dull.

Well, "naturalism" would not do for "The Scarlet Pimpernel". The only way to make anything of it would be to play every part for all it was worth. To "ham". At first this proved surprisingly difficult to accomplish without producing caricature and we had some hilarious moments at rehearsal after the first reluctance to let go had been overcome.

Out of the laughter, however, came an idea. It is so much easier to restrain and refine an actor's performance when he is giving everything, than to get the whole character out of him in the first place. So we tried some scenes drastically overplayed, the point of each line overstressed, all gestures exaggerated, emotions over-expressed. The script certainly lent itself to the treatment and the result was riotous. True, it was considered an undignified waste of good rehearsal time by one or two sobersides, but we did enjoy the fun.

What is more, at the next trial all agreed that the experiment had left them with something new to enrich the character, and indeed the new life infused into the playing was justification enough. From there on, once the fear of "overacting" had been beaten, it was easier and, I believe we succeeded in building up a full blooded, punchy performance.

Our fears that audiences might not follow us to the Church Hall were soon dispelled, for advance booking was good. The opposition did their best by booking "The Garden of Allah" with Marlene Dietrich "filmed in natural colour"! We sold out despite this and on our opening night I could not resist the temptation to send a messenger (Bunter, who enjoyed it) up to the Carlton with my compliments and would they please lend us their "House Full" board. Promptly came the reply I deserved—sorry, they were using it themselves.

We owed much of the success of the "Pimpernel" to our stage staff. The play had to be kept moving: long waits between scenes would have killed it, but Ken Blackmore devised and operated a detailed scheme which worked marvels. And his team worked marvels for him. The "Barricades" set (exterior) was changed to "The Fisherman's Rest" (interior) in under four minutes, except once and of course, that had to be the night Taunton Thespians came! A line got jammed in a loose cleat high up and it meant fetching a step-ladder to clear it. Nine minutes! I died the death. But a happier memory of that scene-change also lives on. Blackmore himself played the bearded Citizen Captain in the first scene: indeed several of the black gang were on as "crowd", each well placed for his particular task at the change. This time all went well. One of the first moves was to drop the main border, change it to "oak beams" and re-hoist. With Scene II safely on its way Blackmore was dismayed to find he had lost his beard. Feeling the heat, he had discarded it during the change and put it aside for later recovery. Alas it was next seen not only by him, but by the company assembled for a repast at "The Fisherman's Rest" and by the entire audience, floating gently down from the ceiling. He had forgotten to retrieve it before rehoisting the border!

Sixteen hundred people saw "The Scarlet Pimpernel" in five performances, almost capacity. It yielded just over £100 for the British Legion after paying for alterations at the Church Hall and it marked an important milestone in our history. With the "Pimpernel", we established ourselves in the Hall which was to be our theatre for so many years ahead, we founded our Black Gang and started making our own scenery, and we learned a style of acting, more forceful, less restricted, which was to characterise our work in future and which, though perhaps inviting the epithet "ham" from some, certainly yielded a richer harvest than we could have dreamt of—and that was to be within the next six months.

CHAPTER TWELVE

REACHING OUT

It was 1939, and Yeovil Literary and Dramatic Society had a problem.

They were a well-established conventional Society inclined I thought, unfairly perhaps, to spell Drama with a very large D and be a little solemn about it all. As to be expected, they were much concerned in The British Drama League Festival of Community Theatre.

This, I quote, "takes place annually in response to an invitation by the League to Amateur Societies throughout the Country to prepare a short play with special care and submit the result to expert criticism. As a result of adjudication a process of elimination takes place at each stage of the Festival, whereby five plays are chosen to appear in London in the Final Festival. Each of these productions will represent one of the five Areas into which the Country is divided (England Eastern, Western and Northern, Scotland and Wales) and these Areas are again divided into Divisional and Preliminary Festivals."

Yeovil "Lit" thus found themselves in the Central Division of the Western Area and if only they could find enough entrants they could hold a Preliminary Festival in Yeovil. They had always had to travel to Taunton for the Preliminary in the past (and there compete with the Thespians at the very start). A Yeovil Preliminary would be better if only they could stage four plays. They could enter two plays themselves; the local Baptists, Beacon Players, would provide a third, but they still needed one more—and that is how we got roped in. John Wilkins again. It was he who first approached me, expounding on the aims of the Festival with all his persuasive enthusiasm. Again I quote:—"By taking part, Amateurs assert their faith in Drama as being something more than a "passing show", and proclaim their desire to improve themselves in one of the most difficult of Arts. The atmosphere of the Festival throughout is one of friendly emulation, but its fundamental object is to assist the development of the art of the Theatre and to promote a right relation between Drama and the life of the community. It will be seen that the amateurs who take advantage of this test join up with fellow amateurs in a common effort, and each learns from the others as well as from the critic. The audiences find their attitude towards Drama to be quickened, their interest and their own critical faculty to be strengthened" (from the Foreword to the Festival Programme).

All this seemed very much in line with our own aspirations to rise above the "tennis club" approach to amateur theatricals, and the invitation came at just the time in our development when we needed to have our standards tested. The "Pimpernel" had gone all too easily and there was a real danger that we might become too smug and self-satisfied. So, yes, we would make a fourth at Yeovil. It would be our first venture outside Sherborne, and the first public criticism of our work.

I was summoned first to a meeting in Yeovil at the house of Mrs. Atkinson to learn about the organisation and the rules governing the Festival. The Central Division of the Western Area was divided into six groups and the winner from each group, plus the best two seconds, would go on to perform at the Divisional Final. The six groups, covering Gloucestershire, Somerset, Wilts and part of Dorset provided thirty-seven entrants in all. The plays must not run more than 40 minutes. Ten minutes allowed for setting and five minutes for striking scenes, and disqualification for the slightest over-run. The only scenery permitted in addition to the curtain surround, a door-flat, a window-flat and a fireplace. Each entrant to have the use of the stage for one hour on the evening before the Festival. The "host" Society to play first and the others to draw lots for placing. The Yeovil Festival would take place at The Princes Theatre on the 10th March and the Adjudicator would be Mr. C. B. Purdom.

Quickly I made up my mind that we would play a comedy, a little irreverent, something to entertain; to amuse rather than impress, to relieve the solemnity of the occasion. The audience would welcome it, and there was no reason why a little laughter should prove our undoing. And there it was, so easily found, the very first in the volume of "One Act Plays of 1938"—"It's Autumn Now" by Philip Johnson—A bitter-sweet little comedy about a failing actor-manager of a touring stock company and his wife in theatrical digs in a Midlands town at the turn of the century. Six beautifully drawn and cleverly contrasted characters; a simple, sad little story relieved by delightful humour of the kind to appeal especially to lovers of the theatre. Fortunately I was unaware of the one snag which would have impelled me to look elsewhere—forty-four other companies had entered "It's Autumn Now" in the 1939 Festival! None of them, however, from our little bit of the Country.

Elliston Drury, Actor and Gentleman, had no entrance and no exit, for he was on throughout the play. And there is no prize for guessing who intended to play him, but I can swear, hand to heart, that it was not entirely egotism. If we were to come badly out of this our first real "exam" I had to take the responsibility, for our play would reflect the development of my original concept, right or wrong.

I was not quite so full of my own importance, however, as to imagine I could take on such a part and produce the play as well. So—again no prize for guessing to whom I turned. Maurie Welcher liked the play and liked the idea of putting our work up for public assessment by a disinterested expert. We both liked the prospect of renewing the relationship we had known together in "Tons of Money" five years earlier. So he took the job.

We cast the play together carefully. For the actor's wife, patient and long-suffering, herself an actress, but a realist recognising failure—Winifred

Hickson, "Livvy". "Night Must Fall" had brought us the ability to work closely and easily together and this would be important if we were to convey the close bonds of affection, hardly ever expressed in words, which kept these two lowly professionals still struggling on together in adversity. It had to be touching.

For Alderman Pomfrey—"respectability his God"—our "Pimpernel" discovery, Fred Forrest. For his acid, vinegary wife, Cicely Avery . . . Which left two to find.

For Mrs. Duxbury, the landlady, we needed not just a conventional stage boarding-house keeper, but a cheerful kindly little soul, revelling in a secret shared with a generous local benefactor—no "theatricals" ever had to walk to their next date from this town if business was bad . . .

The perfect Mrs. Duxbury had been in our midst all the time, but unrecognised as an actress until "The Pimpernel". R. G. Nicholls had come back to the cast for that and had suggested his wife might play Mère Bogard the loathsome old hag at the "Lion D'Or". They, alone of our company had seen the Fred Terry-Julia Nielson production, and Mrs. Nicholls, despite her inexperience, brought more to Mère Bogard than ever I had seen in the part. No longer young, but petite, gentle, altogether charming, she played the filthy old woman with a roguish fun and sparkle which had won her a great success. Now, with her ability at a Midlands accent, I felt sure we had our Mrs. Duxbury to the life. In the end she was to play the part, in different versions of the play, over and over again on all sorts of stages for a long time to come, including the war years, and however trying and fatiguing the conditions, this frail little old lady never failed us. She was the trouper of us all. She is remembered with the warmest affection.

It is not quite clear how Margery Hall came to be cast in the part of The Lady, but it is important to our story that she was, for it was during the preparation of "It's Autumn Now" and due to her enthusiasm and esprit de corps that we acquired our first lighting equipment, found our first permanent stage electrician, and were provided with readily available transport for our travels.

Margery was never one for remaining in the background or slow to make her presence felt, and immediately on taking charge of the "Pimpernel" properties team she had established herself as "one of the management". It is not surprising, therefore, that when one morning she spotted a small advertisement in the Daily Telegraph offering the effects of a small home-counties theatre she decided we would buy the lighting equipment; she almost decided on the tip-up seats as well, but discretion prevailed. We had talked over our lighting problem many times; fortunately the "Pimpernel" had been undemanding in this respect and Jim Cowan (Y.C.F.) had coped with odds and ends borrowed from Wessex Electricity and the Old Fosterians, but if we were to continue at the Church Hall something had to be done and Margery was not content just to talk about it.

She sent for a list of the gear on offer and if this left her in the dark, having not the slightest notion what "floods, troughs, jellies" and the like meant, she had only to ask her brother Bill. Now W. J. Hall, B.Sc.Tech. was not only Managing Director of Wm. Seymour & Co. Ltd. master-minding their celebrated mineral waters, he was a qualified and able electrical engineer and this, years earlier, would have been his career—in the States —but, alas, for diabetes, a scourge which he bore with remarkable equanimity.

Armed with his sound advice, his newly awakened interest and his generous financial support, Marge first dipped into her own purse and then scouted round a select few of the Players, notably Bewsey Dyke (whose whole family have proved wonderful friends to us) Hugh Sawtell, R. G. Nicholls and some whose names are not known to me, all of whom readily dug deep into their pockets. Off went one of Seymour's lorries on the first of many journeys for us—and the Players possessed their first spots, floods, dimmers ground rows, stands, and a good stock of new jellies—all to be housed at Seymours in Bill's custody. He built the dimmers into a portable folding switchboard, which looked to me, I must admit, a dreadful jumble, but upon which he performed absolute miracles for us for years to come as our Stage Electrician.

And that is the story of one of the nicest things ever to happen to the Players, to be remembered with Bill Brown's legacy and Hugh Sawtell's extraordinary generosity over the years. What prompted it? What was the motivation? Why did Marge and Bill and Bewsey and Hugh and the others want to do it? It is a good question.

Now Maurie could have his autumn sun shining through the grubby net curtains of Mrs. Duxbury's front room, and his slow dusk. The front room was coming along nicely too, for Blackmore was making the utmost of our three permitted flats. He built us our first free-standing doorway, an inch clear of the surround so that it could be slammed effectively without shaking the whole set. His fireplace had a splendid "overmantel" and mantelpiece duly draped and tasselled. The room was to be over-furnished and crammed with bric-a-brac, ornaments and photographs on every available surface. The original idea was to stick them all on and travel them already in place, but that would not work so we countered the shortage of time for scene-setting by making false tops for the table, mantelpiece, sideboard and "what-not". The job of collecting, sorting and setting these oddments was taken by Doris who succeeded Marge as property mistress. Doris had played a small part in the "Pimpernel" (the only one, she said, in which she was ever allowed to look pretty) and had been one of Marge's assistants on props. So this was promotion! Unhappily it was also to be the last work Doris could do with us for eight years, for it was about now that severe spinal trouble set in and she was to spend her life in, first a plaster-jacket then a cumbersome brace. She was very plucky about it.

Maurie produced with meticulous care—how I envied and admired his patience, albeit severe, and his attention to minute detail—and our confidence grew that at least we could gain the approval of the audience, for we had an amusing play. Yeovil Lit. had chosen for their star piece, "The Man Who Wouldn't Go To Heaven" by F. Sladen-Smith, and as second choice, an all-women play about witchcraft, "Druids Ring", with a cast which included as lead Helen Palmer (Lady Blakeney of "The Scarlet Pimpernel"). Both produced by Joan Cowell. The Baptists settled for "The Bishop's Candlesticks", so it would be up to us to provide the evening's laughs and that is what we were determined to do, playing it for all we were worth and perfectly prepared to be pilloried for overacting if we were wrong.

It was in high spirits that we set off for the permitted hour of rehearsal on the stage, but that soon evaporated. Too clever once again, I had chosen to take the last hour, nine until ten, thinking we might get a little extra time with nobody to follow us. Accordingly we arrived at the Princes Theatre, Yeovil at about eight-thirty to wait. And we were still waiting at ten o'clock. "The Man Who Wouldn't Go To Heaven" stubbornly declined to go anywhere else either. The trouble was partly, I believe, that the actor playing the Atheist was also Stage Director for the Festival and so was frequently interrupted. At any rate his passionate declarations that there is no God were repeatedly interspersed with appeals to the Almighty to preserve him from the idiocy of well-meaning stage hands still trying to marshall the various companies' props.

So, at 9.45 p.m. we had to make our debut in the B.D.L. Festival by lodging a protest. Mrs. Cowell and Yeovil Lit. had had the stage since 7 p.m. What rattled us more than anything was the conviction that both we and the Baptists were there only as makeweights. I am sure we were absolutely wrong in this, but it was an impression given strength by the dressing-room chatter. Doris and Mrs. Nicholls, sitting quietly together waiting, were much offended. We got the stage at 10.10 p.m. and by then the caretaker was already making "time please" noises, but he did allow us to stay until 10.30 which enabled us to set and light our dingy front room and try the cues. But we went home a bit upset. Where was this "friendy emulation" we had been told about? However, we knew we had a good little show and the set had looked good. Just one little thing to complete the picture, Doris thought; and next evening we took it with us as our mascot. Mrs. Hall's magnificent aspidistra on its bamboo stand.

So on the 10th March 1939, Amateur Players of Sherborne made their first appearance outside the town, much heartened by the number of folk who came over to Yeovil to support them. George Merrick (whose pleasant unofficious work as our Business Manager and Secretary has gone too long unremarked upon) had arranged a late bus back and it was well worthwhile. This unexpected support made all the difference. The despondency of the previous night quickly gave way to exhilaration and we soon caught the air of expectancy and excitement generated by the occasion. A full house, an audience keen, critical and strongly partisan, and in their midst the discretely illuminated table for the man whose judgement would mean much more to us than we admitted, Mr. C. B. Purdom. We had to do well.

"It's Autumn Now" was the second play on the bill. The rules were seen to be strictly observed—five minutes after the first play ended the curtain was raised to show an empty stage and exactly ten minutes later it was opened again to disclose Elliston Drury rehearsing his death scene in "The Sorrows of Satan". Thanks to Blackmore's ingenuity and some good drill, we had a couple of minutes in hand before the rise of the curtain and I remember them as sheer hell. But once on our way we did well and we knew it. The audience were very responsive and (how I wished we had tried it out in Sherborne first) we talked through a laugh or two—for which we got duly taken to task later. Livvy held them splendidly for the final curtain ("Not a dry eye in the house!") and the applause was generous, we thought. Well, we all knew we could not ever do it better, and in point of fact we never did.

Then the long, long wait. I did not see any of the other plays, nor did I want to, for to tell the truth I was sick with apprehension. Our efforts would not be damned I knew, but kindly condescending encouragement with a little faint praise would be just as painful. In truth, I had been fool enough to persuade myself that A.P.S. were a bit superior, a cut above usual "amateur theatricals" and though no doubt it would do me good to have my dream bubble burst, deflation tonight in this way, in front of this company, was something I did not relish. As I recall, Doris and Maurie Welcher took me for a drink at the Mermaid which was conveniently close, and it was a great relief to be out of it all for a little before returning for the adjudication.

Even then we had to wait longer than we liked, for Mr. Purdom chose to discuss the two Yeovil Lit. plays one after the other because they had been produced by one producer. When he did come to us he first spoke at length about the difficulty for amateurs in the craft of comedy. He suggested the value for exercise of playing both melodrama and burlesque, adding something which has stuck in my memory ever since, "All amateurs seeking to serve a serious apprenticeship to their art should at some time attempt Shakespearean comedy—knowing that, as they must, they will fail." Some three years later we did attempt it and I suppose by good standards we did fail, but it was fun.

When at last he got down to the details of our little comedy, Mr. Purdom was pretty severe I thought; more severe than he had been with Yeovil Lit. and my spirits sank. He liked the play as a choice and he had praise for our setting, with a special mention for the aspidistra (to Doris's delight), but when he came to production and acting there was some quite tough criticism. As for me, after saying that the play hinged on the performance of the actor, he proceeded to give me an awful drubbing, or so it sounded to me. He gave me credit for sincerity and good voice, but apparently my "faults in technique would fill a book". There was one comfort; not one of us was criticised for overacting. Only at the end, in summing up "Dramatic Achievement" did Mr. Purdom relent. Only then did he say that our play had merited detailed analysis on the basis of a high standard of performance; and that was heartening. So was the applause which greeted it!

The Baptists received some warm praise and encouragement for "The Bishop's Candlesticks". Then the verdict. First, "It's Autumn Now". Second, "Druids Ring".

As on other occasions, notably after "Nanette" I was again quite unable to throw my hat in the air and cheer with the others—I simply cannot enjoy success. I was now very conscious of the shortcomings in our show and wanted very much to have another try. I am not sure that the competitive element in the Festival had been very strong in our minds; I don't think we had expected to win, but I am certain I would have been shattered if we had not. Anyhow, the rapture had quickly to be modified, for in our Group Mr. Purdom had seen a play at Frome which he had preferred to ours —"A Piece of China" by the Waverley Players. There was still a chance however that A.P.S. might be invited to play in the Divisional Final as "best second" for we were known to have been marked higher than some firsts in other Groups. Sure enough, some time during the next week George Merrick came to work wearing a huge grin and waving a letter from John Wilkins. "It's Autumn Now" was wanted for the Divisional Final at Taunton Town Hall on 1st April.

If the competitive aspect of the Festival had not much concerned us before, it certainly did now. We knew that at Taunton we would be outclassed by some, but we were determined not to come last in order of merit. In addition to the Frome play, already marked higher than ours, we would be acting with the winners of Gloucestershire R.C.C. and Somerset R.C.C. groups, Salisbury Dramatic Society, Bridgwater Players, Taunton Thespians (a bit daunting) and in a class of their own, Hedley Goodall's Bristol Drama Club, winners for the past two years of the Divisional Final, the Area Final and therefore London Finalists. We had to work.

And for three weeks we did, trying hard to heed the criticism and advice we had received in Yeovil. I am not convinced that we improved much but we did get a little stale and tired of trying. Then, three days before the the event and for the one and only time in my life, I lost my voice—completely—not a sound. It was nothing but sheer panic. Dr. Jack thought it vastly amusing, gave me something to suck, something to gargle, told me not to try to talk for twenty-four hours and, above all, not to be such a fool. So I did not have much to do with the final preparations; Bill Hall drove me to Taunton for rehearsal in silence and I whispered through my part.

With the Thespians as hosts, our reception was cordial and all the Festival arrangements ran smoothly. Eight plays—four for the matinée, four in the evening. We were to play third at the matinée, immediately before Bristol Drama Club. The adjudicator was Mr. F. Sladen-Smith. Yes, the author of "The Man Who Wouldn't Go To Heaven". Yeovil Lit. with an eye on the Divisional Final, had either made a crafty choice of play or they had decided to live dangerously. We had little hope, for judging by the tone of his own plays he was unlikely to go much on our choice.

Came the day and the performance. Taunton Thespians opened with Act I of "Tovarich"—an extract, not usually favoured—a slender hope for us, but I had seen them in the whole play and knew their standard. Second Bridgwater. Then us. My throat still hurt a little and my voice sounded very peculiar to me, but we got through without trouble and were well received.

Then came Bristol—to sweep the board from the very moment they arrived. They had an original play written by Cyril Roberts specially for them, "The Roll of the Drum". The scene, a canvas alley-way leading to a circus ring. The cast of sixteen included really skilled tumblers, a midget, and a juggler, headed by some of Bristol's top actors, Rosie Jacobs, A. E. Colston Ball and, of course, Hedley Goodall who was also the producer. For off-stage effects they had brought a twin-turntable panatrope and a coach load of Bristol Grammar School boys for the circus crowd. Their lovely new colourful costumes had been specially designed and executed by Rosetta Ltd. (I am not sure, but I believe that was Rosie Jacobs' firm). Even allowing for the fact that they were old hands at Festivals and at the top of the tree, the absolutely professional efficiency with which they moved in had us gaping. There was an air of superiority, almost of condescension about their work which told us plainly that Bristol had come slumming. The Divisional Final was a necessary preliminary on their way to London. Yet off-stage, in the dressing rooms a nicer crowd of companions and fellow enthusiasts would be hard to find.

We all changed quickly and raced round to see the play. They had most cunningly arranged the curtain surround and added striped awnings to indicate the way-in to the ring; one side dark and gloomy; opposite, the brilliantly lit ring entrance with changing sweeps of colours, the band, the ringmaster, the applause, "oohs" and "aahs" of the boys. It was impressive indeed. No more so though than the appearance of Hedley Goodall as the star of the circus, the trapeze artiste. Tall, bearded, magnificent in his flowing cloak he dominated the scene and the play. The plot was melodramatic and effective but, in a lesser production, a rather thin story on a hackneyed theme, as we were to discover a couple of years later. As presented by Bristol Drama Club though, it was great entertainment and a splendid climax to the matinée. Our effort must have passed completely out of people's minds, we decided.

We saw all the four evening plays; they were all good and we enjoyed them with the rest of the audience, but though we gave at least two of them best, Thornton Wilder's "Queens of France" by Salisbury D.S. and Frome's "A Piece of China", we did feel, all of us, that we had not disgraced the occasion.

Then the adjudication. As expected, Mr. Sladen-Smith ignored the humour in our play, describing it as "clever, bitter and painful". Again we got credit for sincerity and understanding. I appeared rather young for the part but—the joke of the evening for us—had a good voice! Then came the "overacting" bit, although it was only poor Cicely Avery to whom the word itself was applied. To me—"Did an actor of the day, however seedy and spent, behave in private life as he did upon the boards?" It was a point. Of Fred Forrest's Mr. Pomfrey, Mr. Sladen-Smith had this to say, "Extra-ordinarily well acted. Hardly ever have I seen an actor make so much of a part". It was the highest praise accorded to any actor that night. On the whole we had come out of it better than we had expected and as we waited while five more plays were reviewed, it became clear to us that we were not too badly placed. "A Piece of China" was quite roughly handled, we were not at all sorry to hear, and by the time Mr. Sladen-Smith put down his notes at the end our excitement was intense—and with good cause.

The two companies to represent the Central Division at the Western Area Final at the Victoria Rooms, Bristol on 29th April would be Bristol Drama Club in "The Roll of the Drum" and Amateur Players of Sherborne in "It's Autumn Now".

It was quite a moment. Even Maurie permitted himself the tiniest sug-gestion of emotion as we shook hands, with the roars of applause engulfing us. I have a blurred memory of cheers coming from the middle of the audience and of Bewsey standing on a chair. For me—childish, no doubt, but surely it must be plain by now, how much the Players meant in my life —for me it was overwhelming, the culmination and justification of our efforts over the past five years. We were not just a local show now. Now A.P.S. had some standing in the West of England. The congratulations were generous from everyone, none more so than from the Bristol folk who assured us of a warm welcome there on 29th April and promised us they would "show us the way round".

Four weeks. We agreed to rest, to forget the play for three of them and then work hard. Meanwhile, as details of the Western Area Final be-came known, we thoroughly enjoyed some nice publicity. We would be one of seven companies selected to represent one third of England. Sherborne would be the smallest town in the whole country still to be represented in the Festival. We would be sharing the programme with the best from

Birmingham, Leicester, Hereford, Bristol, Bournemouth and Plymouth. Mr. Richard Southern would be the Adjudicator and Sir Barry Jackson was coming fom Birmingham to present a trophy to the winners and send them on their way to London.

No nerves this time; as I remember, our mood during our week of preparation was one of excitement, almost of celebration. We had done all we could and this experience was to be our prize. The only doubt was how far to heed Mr. Sladen-Smith's comments and make Drury and his wife less theatrical off-stage, and we decided to subdue the mannerisms a little. Of more concern, at least to me, was the cost of it all. The expenses allowed by B.D.L. were rather more generous for the finals than for the preliminaries but they did not go far to meet our personal outgoings and I, as ever, was hard up. The problem of staying overnight did not arise though because Doris and I, with the two children could stay with Grannie in Bath.

Considering there were only six in the cast we were quite a big company to move around, but all went well. Seymours moved the flats and furniture etc. (and we found we were in the minority in travelling our own), the stage was waiting for us and the welcome was warm from everyone, officials, theatre staff and other companies. The big shots had been there all day rehearsing and it was impossible not to get caught up in the exciting festive air of the occasion at once. The one thing which sobered us up and for which we ought to have been better prepared however, was the vast acreage of the Victoria Rooms stage. Our little "front room" seemed to consist of bits and pieces each separated by miles of empty floor, and to cross from one to another on cue, one felt a strong desire to break into a trot. Voices too had to be enlarged, for we were in a bigger theatre than ever before. So our hard, concentrated rehearsal left us all feeling a little uneasy and out of our depth.

One company, from Hereford, did not rehearse on the Friday night. They arrived in a rush on Saturday morning and set about borrowing props here and there in what appeared to be something of a fluster. They were giving a first performance in England of a new American gangster play requiring five scenes—in forty minutes! Could they please borrow our aspidistra? Doris was outraged, but it was all in the spirit of co-operation and "friendly emulation" so we could not refuse.

Again there were four plays for the matinée but this time we played second. Bournemouth opened with an Essex Dane, "The Veil Lifts", then Sherborne, then Hereford, with Bristol to finish. I dressed with Hedley Goodall who had that morning suffered a bereavement in the death of his mother, which saddened his whole company and made for a subdued air in the dressing-room. I should add that he gave a magnificent performance in the best tradition of the theatre.

Our play went well, after a quieter beginning than before; maybe the matinée audience were not sure that laughter was quite the thing for such an occasion, or more likely we took time, Olive Nicholls and I, to accustom ourselves to the great open spaces on stage and in front. However, we won them over and at the end our curtain call was all we hoped for. We changed quickly and joined the audience to see our aspidistra make its second appearance of the afternoon. And there it was, our mascot, really working for us, on a table stage centre completely masking one of the speakers, to the unkind and unseemly glee of us all.

Again, "The Roll of the Drum" was great. Immaculately played, staged and directed, it was a perfect demonstration of how a rather trite little story can be built up to a gripping, spectacular piece of theatre.

At tea we placed ourselves third, possibly second, with three more to come.

The evening audience were easier we thought. Nor did we now have the monopoly of humour in the programme; Leicester opened with a delightful send-up of a drama festival, complete with adjudication and the downcast company in their dressing-room afterwards. "Dirge Without Dole"—the title should have warned us, but it took quite a while before we, the audience, realised it was a leg-pull. Well, Sherborne had to concede that one. We were now fourth.

Next came Plymouth with a rather obscure play about the boy Chopin with nice period atmosphere and a plot which I could not follow. Obviously aimed at the highbrows, it might leave us behind. Now fifth, perhaps fourth, but in any case we were not too badly outclassed.

Finally, Birmingham in a shocker of a play about a woman dying of cancer. Morbid, depressing, it was intended to shock and it did. In 1939 cancer was a word never used on the stage, as was forcibly pointed out in one of the final speeches. The play was, however, intensely and sincerely acted and could well earn good marks.

Then Mr. Southern—and he kept his secret very close until the end. He did not like any of us very much nor disclose any particular preference that we could discern from his comments on our efforts. "It's Autumn Now" got what we had dreaded at Yeovil—faint praise. "An enjoyable performance." Elliston Drury "needed more largeness of manner. Edna, his wife "should have had the largeness of style of the actress"—so we had been wrong to heed Mr. Sladen-Smith after all. In general the adjudicator was complimentary to us in very brief terms—setting—very good, props—very good, lighting—good, costumes—good, make-up—good, production—well handled, team work—good, grouping and movement—fair, climax—good, etc., etc. We got very little from it, nor did the other companies in turn, and one could sense a growing impatience in the audience as Mr. Southern ploughed on. At last he was done. He sat down and passed a slip of paper to the Chairman. A moment later Sir Barry Jackson was on his feet to announce the winner and to present the Boughton Chatwyn Trophy—to Hereford.

John Coe, Theatre Critic of the "Evening Post":—

DRAMA AWARD THUNDERBOLT

"Adjudicator Richard Southern chose the Hereford Players' production of 'This Earth Is Ours' as the winner of the B.D.L. Western Area Final. When Mr. Southern's choice was made known, the packed audience gasped. To the great majority it came as a thunderbolt and none perhaps were more surprised than the winners themselves. For my part I was staggered. Quite frankly I would have put this offering, if not on the bottom rung of all, then in the last place but one . . . I have absolutely no axe to grind in this matter at all. If I had been adjudicating my choice for the National Final would have lain between Bristol Drama Club's 'The Roll of the Drum' and 'It's Autumn Now', Philip Johnson's comedy staged by Amateur Players of Sherborne. Forced to decide, my vote would have probably gone to the latter. I am at one with Mr. Southern in praising the ingenious arrangement of the curtains in the Bristol Club's opening, the extraordinarily good 'noises off' and the clever character work and Hedley Goodall's brilliant performance, but 'It's Autumn Now' with its atmosphere of theatrical 'digs' of forty years ago was so realistically caught as to be well nigh the real thing. Sherborne's select group of players made this for me, the most enjoyable play of the Festival."

John Bennett, The Evening World Dramatic Critic:—

AUDIENCE SHOCKED

"There's one thing about these Area Finals: you're usually sure of a first-class dramatic sensation. We had it this year in an award which surprised 100 per cent of the audience and shocked 90 per cent . . . Had I been adjudicating I should have had a hard job to choose between the vigorous performance of Hedley Goodall's Bristol Drama Club and the polished comedy characteristics of the Sherborne company."

The News Chronicle paid us the compliment of publishing only one photograph to cover the Festival—a "Museum Piece" pose of "It's Autumn Now" under the caption:—

APPLAUSE THEIR REWARD

"The decision of Mr. Richard Southern that Hereford Players had won the final of the Western Area brought applause from the Hereford supporters, but was received in silence by the remainder of the audience. The Amateur Players of Sherborne are to be congratulated on 'It's Autumn Now'. The acting by the small cast deserved the applause of the audience and the praise of the adjudicator."

Officially we were placed third and awarded a Certificate of Merit (now in Joy's keeping) and I believe that at best that was about right.

Bristol were certainly better and so I think were Leicester. At any rate, we came home very happy indeed from what had been a great adventure and a very valuable experience.

It remained only to celebrate. We had not yet played "It's Autumn Now" in Sherborne, so whilst some of us had been engaged in travels, the home team had been preparing Sherborne's first Theatre Festival. Frome, with "A Piece of China" and Yeovil, "Druids Ring" combined with us to fill the Church Hall on 4th May, six days after the Area Final. Free now from the tensions of competition and adjudication we had a joyous evening and a great reception. After the performance we entertained our visitors to a riotous supper at The Half Moon during which Bewsey, as Mr. Slate'em-Stiff gave an adjudication which completely demolished any pretensions we might have had as to our own prowess.

We were all set now for the big one in the autumn—J. B. Priestley's "The Good Companions". Sixteen scenes (some could be combined, others inset) and an Austin 7. Ken Blackmore was sure it could be staged. We would work hard for two to three months from the first week of September.

But no. That week is remembered for other things. Handing out gas-masks, "de-bussing" (what a word) frightened little children taken from their homes in London, six Grenadier Guardsmen run down by a bus and killed in the blackout in Newland . . .

CHAPTER THIRTEEN

SERVICE

It was, by any reckoning, a crazy Christmas. We all knew the war would bring many odd experiences, mostly unpleasant, but never in our wildest dreams did we imagine our lives would be brightened for us at the Festive Season of 1939 in this topsy-turvy way. It had seemed so certain that the Players would have to disband "for the duration". The Church Hall like every other available building in the town and around, had been requisitioned. The call-up was, and would be progressively absorbing the younger ones, and the remainder were too heavily engaged in extra-curricular duties for amateur theatre. No A.P.S. now—it was A.R.P. or A.F.S. or the "specials" and soon it would be Home Guard (via L.D.V.).

Yet here we were, on Christmas Day, working more closely together perhaps than ever before, striving frantically to get on to the stage in the School Gym that night a pantomime which for absurdity and incongruity outdid the very meaning of the word itself:—"Cinderella" with a chorus of fairies comprising sixteen Army officrs, a Colonel as Buttons, and a Peer of the Realm as the Wicked Baron Bren; all prancing about at the command of 7014444 Private Batty!

It all began with a copy of Picture Post. On the very day the bank accounts came from Guildford and we knew that the 1/5th Queens Royal Regiment were to be billeted in Sherborne, there they were, featured in Picture Post with a series of photographs taken when they had been under canvas "Somewhere in England"—a battalion of territorials who had suddenly found themselves mobilised for war. The cover of the magazine featured one of the battalion's unusual assets, their talented amateur band, and it was this picture which caught my eye and set me thinking. I talked to Blackmore and Bewsey and Marge: what a good idea it would be to welcome the "Queens" to Sherborne by providing a setting, a properly lit stage with curtains and, perhaps one or two supporting acts so that they could present their own show to their own men to better advantage than, according to Picture Post, had been possible so far.

It worked. Within three days of their arrival we had the Church Hall packed with what was for us a new kind of audience, noisy, generous, surprisingly discerning and sometimes vociferously critical. Bewsey and I opened the show with some casual chat in front of the traverse, looking together at Picture Post, saying what a good idea it would be if ever the 5th Queens did come to Sherborne etc., etc. Then, as we talked, the first distant beat signalled the fade-out and, (very quietly to begin with), the strains of "Roll Out The Barrel" swelled up with the lights to big applause from the troops for their own band, staged as effectively as we possibly could. Our very first Troop Show was on its way. The first of how many? Two hundred? Three hundred? Over the next four years or so we lost count.

The 5th Queens remained in Sherborne through most of the winter and became quite part of the community. There will be many memories of friendships, and of romances, forged then. Doris and I found we had adopted three inseparable members of the band, two trombones and the drummer: Bob, Syd and Batty. Bob had been formerly a Regular Army bandsman and was the "card" of the trio. Syd's name, Sydney Sagar, is now well-known in the world of serious music both as a conductor and composer, and is often seen on T.V. screens amongst the music credits. Gerald Batty was a great character. He was the son of the Bishop of Fulham, a classical actor, experimental producer, occasional fifth percussionist for symphony orchestras and a dance band drummer. He was also a delightful chap, regretful of his reputation as the most inefficient and slovenly soldier in the battalion and quite unable to explain however he became a territorial at all, let alone a medical orderly. It was Batty who received an intimation that officers of the battalion would entertain the men on Christmas Day with a pantomime, and that he would produce it. It was a tough assignment.

I found him a Clinton-Baddely "Cinderella" to work from, and A.P.S. undertook to stage the show, help with costumes and provide the girls. Pat Shaw was "Cinders" and Betty Shaw "Prince Charming". The Fairy Queen was Peggy Merrick (come back Peggy—all is forgiven) and every officer in the battalion was roped in to complete the company. Margery Hall as wardrobe mistress, Ken Blackmore scenic effects and I as stage manager got programme credits, but many more of us worked on the show as and when our various duties permitted.

And there lay the snag; our various duties, military and civil, did not permit, and with two days to go we needed another week at least. Col. Palmer would not hear of postponement, and I can only describe Christmas Eve, late into the night and all Christmas Day as a theatrical nightmare never to be forgotten. The trouble was, I expect, that we took it all too seriously; or the Players and Gerald did. The band remained phlegmatic throughout, but to the officers of the 5th Queens it was all part of the Christmas party, and that had started for them well before the final rehearsal.

It was chaotic. I felt so sorry for poor Batty who couldn't depend even on his close friend Bob to see the urgency of the situation. Despatched to find two kitchen chairs and a rolling-pin for the Ugly Sisters' act, he came back two hours later with only a bag of chips and a tipsy young woman. My own treasured memory of that night is of Marge, knee-deep in crepe-paper ballet skirts and tow hair ringlets, looking distinctly warm, striving splendidly to attire sixteen very masculine fairies amid much ribaldry. She showed great strength of character.

Yet in performance "Cinderella" was no fiasco. Admittedly the rather special audience were in a generous mood and went a long way to make the show, but there was genuine talent and very hard work behind it all. The girls rose to the occasion splendidly, their songs and dances, their touch of "glam" had just the right appeal, and they also did much to keep the plot going. To an audience who did not know of the Shaw twins, Cinderella's transformation from rags to princess was nothing short of magical, and the mirror dance which quickly followed (a lightning change for Pat) and which at its end gave the trick away, can never have had a bigger ovation.

There was a big reception also, but of a different kind, for Major Lord Sysonby as the Bad Baron Bren. He was roundly booed on his every appearance and appeared to enjoy it, glaring back at them through his customary monocle with perfect sang-froid.

The tour de force however, was the much rehearsed ballet. Sixteen muscuar fairies in tin hats, blonde ringlets, ballet skirts and army boots in a perfectly drilled routine, and never a hint of burlesque. What Batty had got them doing was in fact a very fine example of marching and counter-marching in changing formations, with absurdly incongruous hand movements. It absolutely delighted the men, who demanded encore after encore; and Jack Lacey, conducting the band quickly got the idea, giving encore after encore —at the double and ever faster and faster, until no officer was left with a breath in his body. That at last brought a smile to Gerald's face. Private Batty was getting his own back. Pro-tem anyway.

We gave the show again on Boxing Day for "Friends of the 1/5th Queens" and it was packed. At the end, Col. Palmer, still in his "Buttons" suit, made a heart-warming speech of thanks to the people of Sherborne for the friendship and hospitality the troops had found amongst us. Words echoed years later in the official history of the Queens Royal Regiment: "The inhabitants of North Dorset . . . warmly welcomed them and did everything possible for their comfort and amusement, so many permanent friendships and even alliances were made."

Unexpectedy, the "Queens" stayed with us until early Spring, their intended posting to Finland in February, to help the Finns in their war against Russia having been thwarted by Sweden, who would not allow troops to cross their country—much to the relief of many! But in April they embarked for France and by the time the Germans invaded Belgium they were already near the frontier at Armentieres. They advanced into Belgium on the first day of the blitz to a war—and a war record—surely equalled by few. The battalion went into action for the first time on the 20th May 1940, and during the next eleven days suffered many losses in the retreat to Dunkirk. Of our "Cinderella" cast alone, 2/Lt. Hopkins was killed, Capts. Neale (Corporal Fairy), and Watson (Songster), 2/Lts. Jenkins (Attendant Sprite) and Carpenter (Assistant Fairy Queen) were all wounded, Col. Palmer slightly. Capt. Merriman (Sergeant Fairy) was awarded the M.C. and later the D.S.O. "The Bad Baron" Major Lord Sysonby, in charge of the Battalion's

Carriers won the D.S.O. for "hotly engaging the enemy and pushing right into their lines".

Reorganised in England, the Battalion went first to guard the coastline along The Wash against invasion and then to "Hell Fire Corner", with Margate's Wonderland as a parade ground. Here they suffered more casualties, including the loss of another of the "Cinderella" ballet—Capt. Chaldecott. (Here aso they reformed the band, after having lost all their instruments in France together with some "loaned" to them by Sherborne School.)

On the 24th May 1942 they embarked for Africa and subsequently joined the 7th Armoured Division—The Desert Rats—remaining with them until the end of the war, fighting all the way from Alamein to the final attack on Tunis, the famous landing at Salerno and on across the Plain of Naples. Captains Berdoe-Wilkinson and D. U. Clark (who had won an M.C. in France) were killed in Africa and Major R. E. Clarke (Sir Ayebout Turn in the panto) died of his wounds there.

In December 1943, the Battalion returned to England to prepare for the Normandy Invasion and landed in France again on "D Day" + 2 to fight in the battles round Caen. On the 28th March 1944, they crossed the Rhine and fought their way into the ruins of Hamburg where they stayed to the end. In July 1945 they moved into Berlin and in the Victory Parade "marched past Winston Churchill with Colours flying bayonets fixed and the Band playing the Regimental March 'Braganza'."

So with very proper pride, writes Major H. B. Watson who had sung in "Cinderella" and to whom I am indebted for this potted history. He adds, "I wonder if the people of Sherborne in 1939/40 realised what a famous battalion-to-be they nad in their midst". Remembering my friends Batty, Sager and Bob, I could only answer, "No, and I don't think the troops did, either". Some have greatness thrust upon them. But great they were, nevertheless.

To this day Sherborne School preserves a Silver Bugle engraved with the crest of the Queens Royal Regiment presented on the suggestion of Lord Sysonby and Major Watson. I wonder how many of those who see the bugle know the story behind it. Carefully preserved also is my programme of "Cinderella". I see it more as a Roll of Honour really.

* * * * *

Clearly, it had been a good idea for A.P.S. to do the donkey work of providing and furnishing a stage and lighting it, then taking a back seat and supporting the troops in putting on their own show. We were to do it again; sometimes also for touring companies. One such effort was to lead, some years later, directly to great adventures for us. This was a visit to entertain troops in Sherborne by the Thirteen Players from Bristol in "The Lord of The Manor", produced by John Bennett. Drama Critic of the Evening

World who had so liked "It's Autumn Now". We did our best to stage the play adequately, found the props and so on, and all the Thirteen Players had to do was to come and act it, which they did, with Bennett himself in the lead, very effectively. We gave them some supper at The Half Moon before their journey back to Bristol and it was then that John suggested we ought to be linked with Brisol Wartime Entertainers, which he organised with the backing of his paper. It never became more than a very loose association and a very friendly one, but it did gain us some precious petrol coupons; much needed, for by then our work had widened in scope. We now had our own troop show on the road, "Wartime . . . — Variety" and had opened the least spectacular chapter of our story; one which nevertheless can be looked back upon with rather more justifiable pride than perhaps any other.

The audience at that Boxing Night "Cinderella" had included an honoured guest, His Grace the Duke of Norfolk, no less. His Grace was then a Major and the P.R.I. of the 4th Royal Sussex Regiment, who were stationed in small units spread around several villages near Sherborne. Could we not muster some kind of concert party to provide a simple entertainment at each village in turn? We could try. Where could I be found? At Lloyds Bank.

It was left at that, all a little vague, but within a few days a Capt. Thompson, Entertainments Officer of the 4th Sussex came to the office and asked to see the Manager. This call was significant, for it brings into our story the man who not only set the variety shows on the way that day and proved a great support to the Players in the years ahead, but was one of the key figures in forming them into a conventional society when the time came. He was also, I am sure, the strongest single influence in my banking career. I owe him more than I can ever express.

In 1939, on the early and unlamented retirement of Mr. Gobey, F. H. Brooks had come from Wincanton to manage Lloyds Sherborne Branch. One of his first actions was to gain a well merited and long overdue promotion for Peter Caines to be Manager of South Molton, and he took over from him the Treasurership of the Players. A strong dynamic personality, coupled with sound judgement, an eye for essentials and an impatience with pettifogging detail made him, for me, the ideal Manager and he taught me all I ever knew that was worthwhile about Branch banking. He could, of course, have climbed very much higher up the promotion ladder had he wished, but he refused to leave Sherborne and all it came to mean to him. "Harry" or "Brookie" to his friends—he was "Sir" to me until the day he died, although by then I suppose I was technically his senior, a fact that I owed entirely to his training and his influence over me. If Brookie had told me to stand on my head in the market-place because it was good for me I would have done it. (As it was he made me give up smoking cigarettes overnight—simply by a word or so.) I was his Chief Clerk for six years and never recieved a word of praise although I was made sharply aware of my shortcomings. Yet no man ever had a better boss or a better friend.

Brookie had been extending generous hospitality to troops from the outset, so it is not surprising that Capt. Thompson was warmly received, nor that soon after I had been summoned to join them, all my qualms about raising available talent, the difficulties of transport, lack of free time and so on were swept aside and "Entertaining the troops" was on for A.P.S.

Odd that at the very time we might have staged "The Good Companions" we should, in fact, be forming a Concert Party ourselves. It took me back fifteen years to my early efforts in Bath; with, for me, one big difference. There could be no question of returning to the role of stand-up comedian—because I couldn't. It was not a matter of inclination; I had lost the art of it, somehow.

I had to turn the clock back twelve years, to my first concert in Sherborne, for a start in finding artistes—to Redvers Courage, tenor; Wilby Shaw, popular pianist; the Shaw Twins, dancers; Bill Brown, dialect comedian. From A.P.S. we could add to these, Peggy Merrick, soprano and light comedienne; Bewsey Dyke, compere and comedian and (perhaps the brightest, God-giving, inborn talent of us all) Mervyn Davies, lightning cartoonist.

It was enough to begin with, particularly as we were resolved to maintain our theatrical standing by embodying in the programmes whenever possible a one-act play and some review sketches. For the same reason we were determined to dress the stage somehow wherever we went, a curtain surround, a spot-light or two. It would all help to keep the shows A.P.S. shows and, incidentally, to keep A.P.S. afloat when otherwise the war might have sunk us altogether.

The work of organisation fell to Margery, Bewsey, Blackmore and me, whilst Brookie did much in arranging transport, always driving his own car and enlisting the help of friends; W. A. Ffooks (or Mrs. Ffooks), Capt. Luxmoore and many others. Thanks to Seymours we could carry some props; Jimmy Green and Whittaker of their staff drove the lemonade lorries through the blackout to villages around Sherborne over and over again for years on end.

This then, with Blackmore, Bunter, Philpott and Bill Hall to stage the show and a shortened version of "It's Autumn Now" to fill out the second half was the first "Wartime . . . — Variety", and it went on, I think, at Thornford, followed by Yetminster and Leigh, none of us then having the slightest inkling of the future scope of our undertaking, nor the length of the run. For this was during the phoney war which wasn't going to last long anyhow. We were still going to "hang out our washing on the Seigfried Line" and September 30th 1940 was not yet a significant date in Sherborne's history.

Two things were clear from the start: our reception justified the effort, ensuring further demands, and secondly we could not rely on having the same company twice following, because of other duties. This particularly affected the play and the play was popular, so we decided to learn some more one-acts, and of these the permanent stand-by became "Mr. Hackett's Alibi" with a "transferable" cast. Mervyn tells me the company never knew whom to expect as Hackett; Bewsey Dyke, Fred Forrest or me. (Margery still has her copy autographed by the Duke of Norfolk.) "The Dear Departed" was worked hard for some time and later on we essayed "The Roll of the Drum" with Hugh Sawtell in Hedley Goodall's part, but I was never really happy about that one. It needed much more than the very simple setting we could give it. "It's Autumn Now" remained our favourie for sentimental reasons and we never changed the cast. When Winifred Hickson left Sherborne, we said farewell also to the play.

Departures, permanent and temporary, immediate and pending, posed the most pressing problem and called for urgent recruiting, but in this there was no difficulty. In fact it fell to me to dissuade a number of eager volunteers, an embarrassing task which I hated. It was exhilarating though to discover how much genuine talent there was around, some already established entertainers, some awaiting an outlet. From Wincanton came Chaff and Jeff, cross-talk comedians who proved sure-fire winners and each of them a good single act when the other could not come. From the staff of my old school, Shaftesbury came Geoffrey Scalbert, an astonishingly clever conjurer who used the minimum of props and whose sleight-of-hand was wizardry indeed. Geoffrey had developed his art to a high pitch of perfection for its own sake, without any very ambitious ideas in the way of public presentation, and he never ceased to appear surprised at the gusts of applause his act earned him.

It was nothing short of a brain-wave that inspired me to enlist an old friend from my earliest days in Sherborne who was not a stage entertainer at all but who was to prove one of our biggest hits with troop audiences until we lost him to the R.A.F. Jack Wiltshire (Jim to football fans because his initials are J.M.) was a famous soccer referee of international standing. He had not then refereed the F.A. Cup Final (that was 1947) nor had his book "Play to the Whistle" then been published, but he had been much in the public eye for some years and possibly some of his success in our troop shows was due to recognition of a familiar figure from home surroundings and happier times. Jack's friendly, outgoing personality, his racy style, his ability to tell stories against himself and his expert knowledge of the game all combined to make his football anecdotes a very popular item.

Of the more conventional sort of concert artistes I am ashamed to admit that some names have now passed from my memory. There was Audrey Collins, a soprano of sweet voice, charming appearance, but a very limited repertoire; Dorothy Gray, who sang at the piano; Kitty Preston, whom the war had brought to Sherborne, a talented and hardened professional who gave a lesson to us all on how to punch over a popular musical number. There was Eve Moore; there were two piano-accordionists, the very young Peter Taylor and the very petite Mavis Gigg (affectionately known as Squeeze-Box Annie) who was nearly invisible behind an enormous instrument—you could just see the top of her head and her feet, but she played like a master. Betty Ballam danced, so sometimes did "Claudia Hallett's Young Ladies" from Yeovil. There were many more and as time went by they were continually changing. I would say that at any one time we could call on up to thirty artistes from whom to build our programmes. And we needed them, for we were kept increasingly busy.

By the autumn of 1940, Amateur Players had become, more than anything else, an amateur variety agency, supplying two or more shows a week wherever we were told to go. We had found an energetic liaison officer or advance booking agent in the person of Lady (Cecilia) Petrie who came to live at Lillington during the war years. Already busy with W.V.S., Lady Petrie had a way of making immediate contact with army units as they arrived in the district and she arranged our dates. Milborne Port, Henstridge, Stalbridge, Marnhull, Sturminster Newton, Longburton, Thornford, Yetminster, Leigh. Round and round we went, on and on, Sandford Orcas, Charlton Horethorne, Haydon, Chetnole, Evershot, Halstock. Mostly small audiences of a hundred or so, some very large, as at Houndstone Camp, and Blandford, and Yeovilton. It may be said with all proper modesty that we gained a reputation for "delivering the goods" and this led not only to repeat after repeat but to ever longer journeys. We travelled as far as Alderholt, Fordingbridge for the Royal Amoured Corps in one direction and to Bradford-on-Avon and Bridgwater in others.

By the end of 1940 my own personal war had been settled for me by the first of two medicals from which, as rather expected, I emerged under Grade IV to remain a civilian. And as if to confirm the finding I went down soon after with a severe bout of pleurisy which kept me out of action for a while. It also gained me the comfortable A.R.P. job of Post Warden at "D" Post, which meant I could sit happily indoors at night whilst others were out in the streets. "D" Post, I should add was at the Mermaid Hotel! (With a gesture typical of them, Alf and Mrs. Collins had given up their private ground-floor dining-room to offer it as a Wardens Post.) We were the envy of the town's Civil Defence.

Maurie Welcher was a Special Constable with a beat which took him past our home in Bristol Road (where he always managed to find a light showing) and up as far as the Mermaid, so we saw a lot of each other. Margery had a key telephone job at the Centre (U.D.C. OFFICE). Bewsey was in the Home Guard, Mervyn too. Everyone was in something. The Shaw twins were soon off to be nurses. Blackmore had to leave us, Bunter and George Philpott joined the R.A.F. But the gaps were filled and somehow we managed to keep the shows going without a break. Admittedly I could never have played my part in organising them but for the extraordinary amount of licence Brookie allowed me during office hours. I dread to think how much Bewsey, Margery and I inflated the telephone bills of Silas Dyke & Sons, Wm. Seymour & Co. and Lloyds Bank, or how much working time each morning was devoted to marshalling the Amateur Players' show for the evening. Artistes, material, programme, staging, transport—experience and repetition taught us how. We soon got to know the whereabouts, capacity, stage dimensions, lighting facilities etc. of every school and village hall for miles around and time evolved for us a fairly set routine.

Once on stage, the shows tended increasingly from the earliest days to revolve around Bewsey's performance. He quickly developed into the ideal compere, with a breezy relaxed approach; and his little sketches and mimes, strongly individual, never too long, works of art in themselves, were perfect programme links as well. "Taking the girl to the Pictures", "Sewing on the Button", "Blowing Out the Candle", "The Chinese Boxing Commentator"—all new, original and very funny, (Unlike much humour of the day, I am told they have stood the test of time too.)

As time went by, Bewsey's influence and authority over programmes increased and latterly he virtually controlled the variety side of the shows. His efforts to get poor old Bill Brown to keep the length of his act within bounds led to quite a running war between them. In his own line of country, Bill was very very good but, unlike Bewsey, he had no idea of brevity. Worse, he liked, if possible, to go on last and that left Jessie Brown to play the National Anthem—in Bill's own good time! Now Jessie was a sensitive and able accompanist and she was, moreover, a Teacher of the Pianoforte, but somehow she had never learnt to play "God Save the King" Her version of it was nothing short of excruciating.

Mervyn G. Davies, Lightning Cartoonist, deserves the tribute of a chapter to himself. Indeed he could probably fill a book with reminiscences of his five years on the road. He himself puts the number of his appearances at much over four hundred, for he worked with the Players, Lady Petrie, a Yeovil group and at Home Guard shows, and once achieved as many as nine performances in one week. His success and the incessant demand for his act lay not only in its novelty and the amusing gimmicks he employed, but for the sheer brilliance of the cartoons themselves, Churchill, Ghandi, Gracie Fields, Chamberlain, Bop Hope, Hitler—any well-known face completed in so few deft strokes; it was a great display of skill.

For years Mervyn had been a valued contributor to Lloyds Bank Staff Magazine, "The Dark Horse" and we had a private treasure chest of his cartoons in the office, (some customers would not have been amused I am sure) and I may say his caricature of me in my new A.R.P. Warden's uniform with its too long great-coat and too-big tin hat, entitled "Target for Tonight" was actionable, to say the least!

I believe he had first adapted his skills to a stage act as far back as

1932, before he had come to Sherborne, and now, with us, he developed it into a highly polished and professional entertainment. He liked to have a musical accompaniment and used to furnish Wilby Shaw or his deputy Bill Fowler with a list of drawings in order that each character could be depicted with an appropriate tune. This was risky, for there was always the danger they might get out of step and Bob Hope would appear to the tune of "Umbrella Man", Ghandi would get "There'll always be an England", and Chamberlain or Churchill "The Indian Love Lyrics" . . . And Mervyn, bless him, was inclined to be accident prone. Albeit he gave great pleasure to thousands.

"Wartime . . . — Variety." On and on it went. 1941, 1942, 1943. "Ladies and Gentlemen, here we are again. Amateur Players of Sherborne present the same lousy old variety show." I was sure I would say it one day.

There is no denying that as time went by it did become a strain for everyone. It must be remembered that before the war was very old we were left with only those who were either getting on in years or were not very sound in wind or limb; that for them the ordinary day's work was all the heavier because of their diminished numbers and that their wartime duties made for short nights. Yet not a single one of our artistes ever backed out. Right through we could rely on unflagging effort from artistes who, as amateurs, could never have known before the weariness and boredom of the long run.

And sometimes they were not even rewarded with success. None of us would easily forget a ghastly Sunday evening at, of all places, the Carlton Cinema, Sherborne, when we were called upon at the last moment to substitute for a special film the troops had been promised, but which was not despatched in time. They had already seen our show and although we did our level best to stage a fresh programme, we could not win. They had been promised a film, they had come for a film, they expected a film, and they did not want us. We had a very rough ride. Well, for seven years or more we had been proclaiming our desire to get away from self-indulgent tennis-club" theatricals and you couldn't get much further away than this. For this was service, selflessly volunteered at a time when "direction" was the order of the day, and as the show continued to hold together year in and year out in all sorts of conditions it may justifiably be said that the Players' banner never flew more proudly, though that did not occur to us at the time!

The sin of pride, if there was any, had been effectively purged by the Evening World one day quite early on:—

" . . . THE GOAD . . . "

"Visitor to Bristol last week was Lady Cecilia Petrie who, from her home near Sherborne, is doing invaluable work in concert organisation in Dorset through the Amateur Players of Sherborne who are now linked in a friendly way with the Bristol Wartime Entertainers.

Bristol playgoers will remember with delight the Sherborne group's brilliant performance of 'It's Autumn Now' in the British Drama League Area Final last May.

Fred Alcock and his company are organising entertainments for the troops as an extra wartime job, and Lady Petrie is—they are her own words!—the 'goad'.

And a good goad too . . ."

Not funny. The dictionary said—Goad—(noun)—"a spiked stick for urging cattle".

For many years now the good works and high office of Lady Petrie have been much in the public eye. Mayor of the Royal Borough of Kensington 1954-56, Alderman, Freeman, Deputy Chairman L.C.C. 1958-59, U.K. Delegate to U.N. Assembly 1959, Whitley Council etc. etc. Her work during the war years was less publicised, but was valuable none the less and so far as her association with the Players went it was of the greatest possible help. But she was no goad. The stamp of her strong personality, it is true, did become impressed upon our shows as time went by and we began to find ourselves sometimes introduced as "Lady Petrie's Concert Party".

In 1942 however came something which not only ensured that the Players would not lose their identity, but which came also as a blessed relief to all of us, if only for a few short weeks, before resuming our "wartime job". That summer came the opportunity to combine a Service Show with our own raison d'etre; for the Royal Naval Auxiliary Hospital had been established in Sherborne.

CHAPTER FOURTEEN

"SUMMER DAYS"

Somewhere along the line there had been another well deserved promotion in Lloyds Bank. George Merrick was given a better job in Devon and so we lost not only our Business Manager but his wife too, the most colourful of all the early Players.

Peggy went out in style. At her last show with us she surprised us all by failing to fly into a tantrum at being asked to go on second whilst Audrey Collins had a more favoured spot later in the programme for the only two songs she ever seemed to bring with her. Peggy was always sent on early—she had the ability and zest to warm them up—and she always protested: we were used to it. But not tonight; for her last appearance, (it was at Leigh), she accepted the position with a sweet smile, handed her music to the accompanist, (whose obvious dismay should have been a warning) and proceeded to a soulful rendering of both Audrey Collins' songs!

Peggy, alas, appeared to love making enemies, causing raised eyebrows, inviting ridicule:—she was the only woman I have known who could wiggle on a bicycle; which she did riding very slowly up the middle of Cheap Street, bowing to left and right, without ever bumping into anything or falling off. But on a stage before an audience she was a different being, the most accomplished amateur comedy actress of my experience.

We missed George in a very different way; only after he had gone did we really appreciate all he had been doing for the Players from the very start. Although glad he had got his promotion I was sorry to see him go; we had started pushing pens together, posting ledgers, as long ago as 1931, the year we had been in "Iolanthe" together, and we had been close friends ever since. Sadly, George was to die quite soon after leaving Sherborne.

There was never any doubt about our next Business Manager. Already closely involved in the day-to-day organisation of our shows, Margery Hall found the job fall almost automatically into her lap and she was to bring to it her own brand of intense enthusiasm and energy, coupled with a fervent esprit de corps.

I like to think it was Margery's idea that we should approach Surgeon-Rear Admiral Cory to see if, as part of the R.N. Hospital's recreational activity, the Staff might care to join forces with the Players to produce a play. That would be romantic indeed, for the idea was to lead to the event which changed the whole course of her life and bring her the greatest happiness.

The response from the Hospital was very encouraging and at an informal gathering at the Mermaid we met quite an enthusiastic bunch of W.R.N.S., Sick Berth Attendants, and—Warrant-Wardmaster B. R. Yaxley, already an experienced entertainer and to the fore in organising the Hospital's social functions.

Our choice of play, if at all practicable, was dictated, for obvious reasons, by outside circumstances. First, we| had no theatre, and this led to the suggestion of an open-air production. In turn that would mean playing during the summer, when, as it happened, there would be less pressure for troop shows, and during school holidays when we might have additional help from School Staff. It all pointed to Shakespearean Comedy, about which, unfortunately I knew absolutely nothing. I remembered all too clearly the adjudicator's exhortation to amateurs on the subject wayback in 1939, and his warning:—"knowing that, as they must, they will fail". Well, now was our chance to try and we would try hard not to fail.

Years earlier I had once been invited to play Benedick in "Much Ado About Nothing" with a Somerset group. Nothing had come of it then but I had read it carefully and now I read it again. Comedy, ideal for a garden, a large cast not depending on any one strong lead, music and dancing for extras. It seemed right for our purpose.

So to the Rev. Arthur and Mrs. Field who had been supporters of A.P.S. from the start, (—Mrs. Field had been a second violin in the "Nanette" band!) and whose home at Greenhill House possessed one of the loveliest gardens in Sherborne. At once they agreed to allow us the use of it and went on to offer us most generous hospitality throughout the lovely summer of 1942. We could not possibly have found a better open-air theatre; spacious, beautiful, its sloping lawns providing a stage and auditorium of just the right proportions, trees and bushes in just the right places—and in the very centre of the town! Better still, it adjoined the Music School, made available to us as dressing-rooms through the good offices of Mr. Picton.

Next, to Westcott House and Geoffrey O'Hanlon. I simply did not know enough about Shakespearean work to tackle the production with any sort of authority, or of speaking verse (of which there is less in "Much Ado" than in most), or the appropriate cuts and so on, but he did, and he agreed to produce. This was the first and indeed the only one of our plays during my days in which we enjoyed the help of any Sherborne School staff; mainly I think, because during the headship of Mr. Ross Wallace there simply was not the leisure during term to give the necessary priority to rehearsal time. But this was out of term, so in addition to Mr. O'Hanlon, in came J. H. Randolph to score a great success as Dogberry and, to my delight, B. J. F. Picton to play the aged Antonio, a small part to which he brought a rich voice and all the strong "presence" we had held in awe across the footlights in Gilbert and Sullivan days.

I cast all the female roles from W.R.N.S. and one of them, Joyce Lloyd-Jones, was a find indeed for Beatrice. High-spirited, possessing a musical voice and good clear diction, she brought a bright intelligence and an infectious gaiety to this most provocative of Shakespeare's heroines.

To my initial dismay, Maurie Welcher decided he wanted to play Claudio, the romantic Young Lord of Florence! And not a day under 50! So what? Irving had played Romeo at sixty-two, and we owed enough to Maurie to warrant letting him have his way. Anyhow it was no worse than casting myself as Benedick, with my legs. (I had to wear two pairs of Long Johns with cotton wool sewn in between to give me some thighs).

The other leading roles fell in fairly simply; Hugh Sawtell, game for anything as usual, became the aristocratic Don Pedro, dear old Fred Forrest took on the aged Leonato, but I was lost for the chief villain of the piece, Don John, and it was a great relief when O'Hanlon agreed to play it himself. After that it was a matter of "all hands". Geoffrey Scalbert, our conjurer joined Warrant Wardmaster Yaxley to do Don John's dirty work for him, Bill Brown as Verges joined J. H. Randolph in command of the Watch, an unruly collection of Sick Berth Attendants and anyone else we could rope in, including George Ford, the hairdresser, J. H. Young (junior at Lloyds Bank) and Mervyn Davies. Mervyn, I must add, had another part also, the Messenger, with two important entrances. Bewsey found the time to appear as a Sexton.

Including "The Ladies" and "The Gentlemen" we succeeded in finding a cast of thirty-four, but we had to search amongst the aged and the very young; hence the first appearance with the Players of a fourteen-year-old, Joy Alcock.

* * * * *

We were off. We could proudly announce:—
AMATEUR PLAYERS OF SHERBORNE, together with SERVING
    MEMBERS OF HIS MAJESTY'S FORCES, present The Comedy of
"MUCH ADO ABOUT NOTHING"
by
William Shakespeare
on behalf of
King George's Fund for Sailors
(Merchant Navy).

The preparation of this play was unique in my experience. Never before or since have I known such a sense of relaxation, relief and restfulness in approaching a production. For six precious, all-too-brief weeks of rehearsals we could enjoy the peace of summer evenings in the Field's lovely garden, doing what we liked doing best. One forgets the interruptions for air raid alerts, the enforced absences, the occasional bad weather as of no real account. Instead, there is a vivid memory of Mrs. Field bearing trays of lemonade drinks for us at "break" and of small groups at ease on the lawn "cueing in" lines for one another. An oasis of calm, a glimpse of sanity, a reminder of values almost forgotten.

Mr. O'Hanlon dealt very gently with us, learnedly pointing the verse, patiently explaining the words we could not understand or pronounce. As "Stage Manager and Assistant Producer" I found plenty to do, but the one never free to take her "ease on the lawn" was our new Business Manager and Secretary, Margery, shouldering her freshly acquired responsibilities with tremendous zest. It is greatly to her credit that although this was our first full length play for nearly four years and remembering all that had happened in the meantime, the machinery for organising the production in the Players' own way moved into action as smoothly and efficiently as if there had been no interruption.

With Harry Brooks she rallied the Subscribers as before, she hired costumes from Doreen Errol, London, and saw to it that we each paid for our own. No adverts in the programme this time, but Sawtells actually gave them to us, so we could still promise that every penny paid for them would go to King George's Fund for Sailors, Margery found seating for the audience, dancing lessons for us; she was everywhere, a busy little body indeed, and a great great asset, then and for the next few years, until her work with us resulted in, and furnished the happiest of reasons for leaving us.

For most of us, however, there was a strong element of self-indulgence about "Much Ado", so it may be said that this play marked our fall from grace, the first departure from our original principles. Or, perhaps it was when we first grew up and were honest with ourselves. True, we hoped to make a profit for a good cause, but without much effort. With no rent or royalties to pay and very few other expenses we could not fail to show a profit even though we did not expect many would come to see us. True, we were helping Service men and women to find an interest for their leisure hours; but first and foremost we were enjoying ourselves in holiday mood and in a leisurely way. I like to think, and I do believe, that afterwards we continued to work hard with a serious sense of duty to our audiences, authors and the art we tried to practise, but we never again returned to the anxious urgency of our first few productions.

One thing, however, we did regain, was the full-blooded, punchy style which "The Scarlet Pimpernel" had taught us. We found too, that the years of working together in variety shows had brought an added toughness and assurance. Now we had to concentrate on finding huge voices to compete with the birds and the breeze in the trees, so it was valuable as well as pleasant to rehearse in the garden whenever we could; but it had to be the Mermaid when wet, or Lord Digby's School, to which we all trooped to learn to dance the pavane and the galliard from Miss Metcalf.

Rehearsals were perforce scrappy and uncertain because of "duties", but that had to be accepted and between us we must each have read for absentees every part in the play. It came as a pleasant surprise therefore, to find it all taking shape so well. Randolph, Brown and The Watch worked up really funny scenes. O'Hanlon, Yaxley and Scalbert developed into most dastardly villains. As for Beatrice and Benedick, Hero and Claudio, the girls may not have been very well served, but we enjoyed it all so much that it may have proved infectious. So by Dress Rehearsal we felt we had an acceptable offering, if nothing more. In the event we were completely taken by surprise at the amount of public interest and by the enthusiasm of our reception. The bald facts speak for themselves.

We had decided on only three performances, Friday and Saturday, 14th and 15th August, 1942 at 6.45 p.m. with a matinee on the Saturday. The evening shows would have to start early because there was no question of artificial lighting and people liked to be in their homes before nightfall. Mr. Lush had kindly told us we might transfer to Foster's School in case of rain. We thought two hundred chairs would be plenty. Tickets would be cheap because, despite the appeal of our cause, money was short. There would be no advance booking because the times we lived in were too uncertain.

All a sad miscalculation. By 6.45 p.m. on the Friday all seats had been taken by early arrivals; others were sitting on the grass in front or standing behind and they were still coming in. We made a late start, unusual for us, not only to get the audience settled, but because Mervyn, who as the Messenger had the opening line, had hidden himself so effectively in a bush just off stage, for his entry that we couldn't find him! Eventually, however, over Horace Hamblin's loudspeakers came, for the very first time, the little scrap of music that was to become our signature tune and would mean so much to us, and particularly to me, in the years ahead.

I had left the choice of music for the play to Maurie Welcher and had expected nothing but Elizabethan hey-nonny-no. For the pavane and the galliard yes, and for some linking passages, but otherwise he was quite unorthodox. There was, for instance, some Elgar—"Wand of Youth" suite. And to introduce the play came this light little tune, the introduction to "At The Dance" from Eric Coates' "Summer Days" suite. Had I been consulted I would have condemned it as out of period and quite unsuitable, and that would have been yet another of my big blunders.

In fact, for no reason that I can explain, I have used it to open nearly every play I have produced since 1942, not only for the remainder of my days in Sherborne, but in Swindon, London, Harrow and Gloucester. It always seemed to find a place in the affections of the company and it pleases me now to think there have been folk spread over a wide area of the Country, and of all ages, who regard it as peculiarly their own, and who hear it occasionally with memories of happy times together. "Summer Days".

On that first night, absolutely everything went right for us; the weather was lovely, still and warm; the air-raid siren was mercifully silent; the performance may not have been of a very high standard but there were no disasters and the audience, easy to please no doubt, were generous to us. We all had a wonderful time.

Then down came the rain. It woke me up and I lay awake for the rest of the night worrying about it. The morning cleared sufficiently to tease us a little, but it was a gloomy little bunch of Players who gathered at lunch-time in the Half Moon to debate the problem. Our minds were made up for us in the end by Dorothy Wicks W.R.N.S. (Playing Hero in the play) who had a contact at the Naval Met. Office, and she came back from the telephone with a forecast of storms.

So, at one o'clock, Horace Hamblin's loudspeakers were put to another use and out came his van to tour the streets announcing that both matinee and evening performances would be at Fosters' School. Out too came Seymour's lorry to move furniture, properties and costumes. We opened on time at 2.30 p.m. to a smallish house, which however, continued to fill during the first half-hour, for it had only just started to rain again and many had gone to Greenhill House.

We had never stepped on to the Foster's School stage before, yet the performance went almost without a hitch and there could have been no better demonstration of the fact not only that Shakespearean staging requires no fixed entrances and exits, but also that our work during the last two years had taught us to adapt quickly and easily.

Yet it was a disappointment to us all, players and audience. So after hastily snatched conferences between scenes and with many qualms about getting extra time off from duties, it was decided that at the end of the matinee I would announce an additional performance on the following Monday in the garden, wet or fine. There would be no charge for admission or for programmes, but a collection at the gate. Would they please spread the news etc. etc.

And that was the night to remember. Our Saturday audiences must have worked hard for us and so did Horace Hamblin and his loudspeakers. The extra performance was even included in the Notices at the Abbey on the Sunday. And the result of it all was the largest audience of the four, who gave at the gate more than we took at any performance. It was a perfect summer evening again and the whole occasion took on the air of a Gala. We enjoyed ourselves as never before.

The biggest laughs of the evening were provided by the only untoward incident. In accordance with accepted practice at that time, our programmes included a footnote:—"Should an Alert be sounded there will be a slight pause in the action of the Play to enable anyone who so desires to leave". An Alert was sounded, just as Redvers Courage (Balthasar) was nearing the end of "Sigh No More Ladies," and obediently he paused—in mid-air! After a respectable wait, during which nobody moved, and after "Winnie" had subsided, he picked up the melody again and solemnly polished off the last two lines to generous applause. Then came the next words of dialogue from Benedick—"And he had been a dog that should have howled thus they would have hanged him." Apt enough, but—the "All Clear" came as Conrade and Borachio were plotting their nefarious schemes, the one in a great state of nerves, the other drunkenly oblivious. No pause this time and over the siren's wail came, "Didst thou not hear something?" "Aye, 'twas the vane on the house"! It became a catch phrase among us whenever the siren sounded for long afterwards. "Didst thou not hear something?"

In the end, "Much Ado", the play we had looked upon as a holiday, a relaxation from work, proved our biggest financial success and we eventually sent King George's Fund for Sailors £156 which, in the currency of 1942, was a lot of money.

Afterwards a chance remark from Mrs. Forrest as we parted stuck in my memory. "You know Fred, you ought to produce "Dear Brutus" one day and give Joy a chance." I knew nothing about the play, but it was nice to know Joy had made an impression.

CHAPTER FIFTEEN

TEN YEARS OLD

Back to the treadmill; all through 1943, well into 1944—"Ladies and Gentlemen, here we are again". Increasingly now we could include "Ladies" in our greeting for we were often playing to civilian audiences in connection with "War Weapons Week", "Wings For Victory Week" or just "Holidays At Home". These War Savings efforts were tiring, hectic and great fun. Tiring especially for those of us engaged in the clerical side of it all, for vast sums of money were pouring in each day from Savings Groups in firms, schools, clubs and villages for miles around, mostly in very small individual amounts, everyone demanding to know the daily total of their particular "subscription to the War Effort", and each out to beat his neighbour. There was a strangely festive air about it all and, though banking routine got reduced to chaos, never have pens been pushed with greater enthusiasm. It did not, however make for careful preparation of our evening shows, which had never been in greater demand. So things did go wrong sometimes.

Every town and village organised a round of socials and entertainments, dances and raffles for these "Victory Weeks" and A.P.S. did their best by undertaking a show a night; and on occasion two shows a night in neighbouring villages, with a shuttle-service of artistes) from one to the other as the programme progressed. Mervyn won't let me forget the night we doubled at Yetminster and Leigh, but through some error we all turned up at Yetminster and nobody at all at Leigh.

It was at Evershot on one of these shows that we suffered our only injury and had to enquire for "a doctor in the house". In his "Herr Restorer—celebrated Latvian pianist" act, Bewsey broke a finger, but in the best tradition, finished the show.

It was also in one of these shows that I was able to fulfil a long held wish to present Sherborne Boys' Brigade Band in a short concert programme conducted by Charlie Parsons, whom I so greatly admired. As a change from leading processions up and down the street, they richly deserved recognition as artistes and the appreciation of an audience. To my delight Charlie was quite overcome by the warmth of the reception the boys got. For this occasion we were allowed the use of the Church Hall and it was like coming home. We played two houses—5.30 and 7.45—both full, and never had our variety show enjoyed easier or more enthusiastic audiences, despite the discomfort of wooden chairs and benches, and no heating.

The year 1944 brought American troops and a new kind of audience. Like the Naval Hospital, the Americans also found us some new artistes, some well-known in their own country, such as Frederick Kahn, the pianist. But this was nothing new; all through the war we had been assisted by artistes from the ranks of the troops we were entertaining. Thus, the popular musical hall duo, "Nosmo King and Partner", appeared with us at Taunton, "Partner" (Jack Watson) being at the R. N. Hospital. There were many more whose names I am sorry to say now escape me—except one, a lance-bombadier stationed at Crundle Court, one Harry Secombe. This was just before he went out to the Middle East and met the other Goons. Mr. Secombe and Bewsey have kept in touch through the years and I am told his shows with us are remembered with affection.

The one recruit from the Forces who was to stay with us and play a leading role in our story was Warrant-Wardmaster Yaxley. Bob joined the Variety Show in a cross-talk act with a colleague at the hospital for which they used to "black-up". This was great until one Sunday when we travelled up to Bradford on Avon (to the very same cinema in which my boyhood concert-party had finally folded in 1926). Here, Bob found, too late, that we were entertaining an audience made up entirely of coloured Americans. And he had to make his entrance through the auditorium!

Bob Yaxley was a good "Heavy" and as such, a lucky find, especially at this time when we were nearing our tenth birthday. I was determined that, if humanly possible, we would celebrate it with a play production. "D" Day had come and gone and though "Lady Petrie's Concert Party" was still kept busy. Bewsey found himself now almost in full control, which left me time to tackle the problem. I turned first to the two old friends who had started the Players with me ten years earlier, Maurie Welcher and John Elliott. Together with Margery and Bill Hall and backed by W. J. Cordy, we approached Mr. Lush to see if we could be allowed the use of Fosters School Hall for the best part of a week during the school term, and to our delight he most generously agreed.

I had a play already in mind, a comedy-thriller by Alec Coppel, "I Killed The Count", and I now had just the right "Heavy" for the blustering, exasperated police inspector upon whom the success of the play entirely depends. For the rest, we hit on the idea, for the first time in our history, of inviting applications for parts. So we called an informal open meeting at the "Mermaid" when we talked about the play, read bits and laid down the work required. The response was good and we made several new recruits who might otherwise never have joined us. Diana Wilcoxson, George Gray, George Spiller—and Lucie Smith, surely the most extraordinary Thespian of my experience. Mention of her name merits a brief pause in our story.

Visitors to the Church Hall may note a small plaque above the inner glass-doors:—"These doors were the gift of the Juvenile Players of Sherborne. Leader: Mrs. Harold Smith." and behind these words lies a most astonishing story of achievement which ought certainly to be told in detail one day, for "Polly's Pantos", as they became known deserve a place in any account of Sherborne life just after the war, and many of the children taking part must remember the experience with pride and pleasure.

Harold Smith had for some years been seeing his "Coldharbour Dairy Farm" diminishing to make way for new estates, but it was still there, keeping and housing that large ever cheerful farmer, his large matriarchal wife and their six children. I believe Mrs. Harold Smith had received no formal education in the Arts, but deep in her capacious bosom the nine muses must have been bursting for expression, for she spared no effort to ensure that all her children should have some musical or artistic accomplishment. And not only her own children.

On her first appearance with us, Mrs. Smith gave little indication of talent, but she did display the most intense involvement in the character of Polly, a chambermaid. Every little speech came forth as a passionate outburst which was, to be truthful, a little disconcerting. Yet in years to come, as Founder and Producer of Sherborne Juvenile Players, Polly, as she was affectionately known to us ever after, was to win the respect and admiration of us all.

It can only have been the intensity of artistic burgeoning and strong personal drive of this astonishing woman that achieved such amazing results once she had made up her mind to produce a children's pantomime. She organised it, she wrote much of it, she selected the music, taught the dances, designed the dresses and supervised their making. Added to her own zeal, this steaming power-house called, inappropriately, Lucie, could get prodigious efforts out of anybody and everybody she bullied into helping her. She held all our stage staff in the palm of her hand and the kids themselves would work for her till they dropped.

A call at the farmhouse presented a picture vividly remembered. The living room absolutely crammed with panto props, partly made costumes, piles of curtains and dress material, heaps of sheet music hastily pushed up to one end of the table to make room for Harold's meal, and in a small clearing, Polly, earnestly coaching two small children in some dance steps—to an audience of chicken on the window-sill, indoors!

In the event, that first pantomime, with daughter Enid Smith as Cinderella, was a sensation and there was never any doubt that the Juvenile Players would become an institution. So they did, for six years after the war. But the mystery remained. How did the Farmer's wife ever learn how to do it? For what it is worth, her father was the Drum Major of the 1st Grenadier Guards and some of her earliest memories were of the Trooping of the Colour—if anything can be made of that!

Whatever the source of inspiration, Polly's Pantos were an astonishing achievement and it is a cause for pride that they sprang from her association with us in 1944 as the maid in "I Killed The Count". Through the years, A.P.S. were to gain several new members who had first interested themselves in the Juvenile Players, notably Mr. H. Day who was such a staunch old friend for so long.

"I Killed The Count" brought into the Players the third of the Dyke family, Elizabeth, and the first of the Brett family, Gerald. Liz had much of her brother's gift for humour and used it in her own sharp brittle style, strongly individual. She was blessed with a striking presence and that indefinable something:—when Liz made an entry, someone had positively arrived. She was to do invaluable work for us.

Gerald Brett headed a family procession, for he was soon to be joined by his wife, Phyllis and his sister Phyl Shelton. Years later they were to be followed by his daughter Margaret, his son Jeremy and his daughter-in-law, Ann—and then by his grandson, John. It is good to know that these family links, reaching down the years from one generation of Players to the next have done much to perpetuate our early tradition; the Halls, the Dykes, the Bretts—and Joy.

Gerald had a rough time in his debut with us; he was murdered three times by three different assassins after three fights, during one of which in rehearsal he lost his denture. Fortunately Bewsey made a magnificent single-handed catch in mid-fight.

The thing that really threatened disaster for the whole play, however, only showed when the time came to lay aside books, for Bob Yaxley either couldn't, or wouldn't learn his lines. It must be acknowledged that his part was most difficult to memorise. And I should know, for I had to prepare to take it over if necessary. No doubt about it, it was a pig of a part. The police inspector was on stage for nine-tenths of the play and as he did nothing but ask questions, nobody ever gave him a cue.

It was at this stage in rehearsals that I fell ill again and Margery held the book for me to keep things going. Now Margery and Bob had not been getting along like cooing doves exactly ever since "Much Ado", when she had blotted her copybook in his eyes by seating his commanding officer, Surgeon Rear Admiral Cory, C.B.E., R.N. and his Lady in the second row instead of the first. Now, with Margery in charge and Robert floundering, feathers really were flying. Stories of terrible ructions came back to me as I lay in bed trying to memorise the part. But on return I had to admit that where I had failed Margery had succeeded: Bob was nearly word perfect and in the end he carried the play with a truly impressive performance.

It was all too clear that there could be no better cause to work for than The British Legion once again and, as in earlier years, two of their local members joined our management, chaired by W. J. Cordy.

John Elliott turned out and repaired some old twelve-foot flats (probably in former use by The Old Fosterians), and made some new doors etc. The end product was a good looking, practical set which might have been made to measure for the Foster's School stage.

Thanks to the Royal Naval Hospital we were able to have a small orchestra once more—(I do so prefer "live" entr'acte music if possible)—this time under the direction of Ron Sheppard, a professional pianist. With him he had Surg.-Lieut. Langmaid (Clarinet), Mrs. Brewster, Hugh Sawtell's daughter, Maureen, Mr. Fiori and Miss Wilkins (Strings) and F. G. Mee (Bassoon). It was an unconventional combination, but very successful and very popular.

Our tenth Birthday Production may be fairly adjudged an accomplished and confident success. In the event Bob Yaxley's performance dominated the play, as indeed it was vital that it should, and the two or three newcomers to our Company surpassed expectations. But for the remainder, both on stage and behind, it was not a question of expectations; Bewsey, Welcher, The Forrests, Davies, Sawtell, Elliott, Marge and Bill Hall—we had all been working closely and continuously together, week in, week out, for four years and the outcome could now be seen in a performance of "near-professional" standard. Now, coming from me, the use of that term certainly calls for explanation.

Welcher has often delivered himself of the judgement that "75% of the producer's time in an amateur effort is spent in teaching actors how to act". I have always maintained that lack of opportunity to practise our art for sufficient time is enough alone to prevent us from ever acquiring the technique of even a poor professional. And even that stricture takes no account of the value of training. Consider as a single example, the constant study and years of practice to which an instrumentalist must devote himself before becoming an acceptable public performer.

The curse besetting the amateur actor is that it is so dreadfully easy to do—badly. "Playing at acting" is an insult to author and audience. Yet even serious amateurs, to whom the theatre means an essential form of self-expression, all, save a tiny number, suffer the crippling handicap of being able to act in public only very infrequently, and then always to the same local, hopelessly indulgent audiences.

And whatever can be done about them? Once in, they seem to lose all discrimination. As if it is expected of them they make a practice now of applauding the set before they have even had time to look at it properly. And as for those exits! Recently (in Sherborne I am sorry to say), I heard applause (which interrupted the action of the play) for a small-part actor going off after a five-minute appearance early in the first act!

These same audiences are not slow to offer criticism, and quite rightly so, for they have paid their money, but the trouble is that it never reaches the appropriate ears. So our earnest amateur, unschooled, inexperienced and subjected to the lavish flattery of friends and neighbours, stands in grave danger of believing he is good. And from then on, all is lost.

In "I Killed The Count", I knew the great joy of directing a company, most of whom had gone a long way in learning their job in the hard school of unaccustomed and ever-changing conditions, ever-changing audiences and continual practice. The result could truly be seen in work of almost professional standard in its precision, attack and discipline.

It could be seen also in the ease with which we could transfer the whole production to Summerleaze School, Yeovil a week later in aid of another war charity, (the first of our "tours"). This one-night stand raised £32 for its cause after clearing all expenses, which left their local committee very happy.

Our four Sherborne performances did very good business too, and lots of nice things were said about us on the last night, when Mr. Cordy, in a pleasant little ceremony, handed a cheque for £110 "on account" to the Chairman of the British Legion Sherborne Branch, Mr. Tom Lowman. The final figure was £134.

* * * * *

I ought now perhaps to write "Finis", because my task, as originally set, is done.

I have set down faithfully the background and circumstances, the beliefs and the events which together went into my concept of Amateur Players of Sherborne—in short, I have explained their origin. I have traced their progress through their first ten years, 1934-44, by which time they were firmly established, had gained something of a reputation and had given away £760. By then, too, the name had come to mean quite a lot to more than a hundred folk who, at some time or other, had been Amateur Players.

Can there be any purpose, therefore, in continuing their story? Indeed, is it possible to do so without becoming boringly repetitive?

I am tempted to try. For one thing, at ten years old we would never have countenanced the idea of changing into a conventional dramatic society and the story of our next three years may do something to explain our later transition. Then, some Players who figure prominently in our history have not emerged. And anyhow, the years 1945-47 were exciting for our Company and do warrant some record.

So for those still interested and, it is hoped, with a little less accent on the first person singular . . .

CHAPTER SIXTEEN

MAGIC IN THE AIR

Mystery, Wonder, Romance. They all went to make the story of 1945 for us. Not surprising, for we were with J. M. Barrie. Not the Barrie of "The Admirable Crichton" or "Quality Street", but Barrie the Mystic, of "Mary Rose". "The Boy David" and—"Dear Brutus".

Some mystery remains to surround the story as I try to tell it thirty years later. We gave nine performances of "Dear Brutus" on four different stages between April 26th and May 19th and somewhere in between came "Victory in Europe"—May 8th. So we must have been working right through the V.E. Day celebrations almost without noticing the event! Further, we were back home in the Church Hall once more when it should have been still in army occupation! Puzzling. Unimportant of course; its just that so much remains unexplained about this astonishing episode in our lives.

Of V.E. Day, I remember only the bonfire on Plum-Pudding Hill. Getting my priorities all wrong again, I was too preoccupied with "Dear Brutus", or it may have been my acknowledged inability to join in celebrations. I do remember thinking though how different it all was this time. People were not throwing their hats in the air quite as they had done on 11th November, 1918. There was now a feeling of relief or deliverence more than anything else. In loss of life, Sherborne had been miraculously spared—I am thinking especially of 30th September 1940—but even so, and even here at home we knew something of war weariness. And now it was over.

For long afterwards I felt ashamed about two periods of the war; first, that I should actually have been on holiday at Charmouth with my family at the time of Dunkirk, when I was only thirty-five, and, second, that I should have paid so little heed to the end of it all, to have felt so little concern for the battle-scarred and the bereaved, as if my world had been elsewhere. All that really mattered to me on V.E. Day was Castle Cary the day after tomorrow in aid of "The Welcome Home Fund".

Now there's another odd thing. Our other charities on this tour were The Royal Naval Libraries and the British Red Cross Society, both of which seemed relevant to the times, but at Castle Cary they must have been very forward-looking. "The Welcome Home Fund" on V.E. Day + 2!

Most puzzling of all though, was the "unconscious foresight" that led us to put on "Dear Brutus", "the play of the second chance" exactly as the war was ending. For so many, this was the time for thoughts either of settling down again or of making a fresh start; a time when so many homes had been destroyed and so many lives disrupted. Barrie had judged the mood of end-of-war audiences exactly. The first production of "Dear Brutus" had been staged in similar circumstances in 1918 when it ran for a

year at Wyndhams with Gerald du Maurier as Will Dearth and Faith Celli
as his dream-daughter, Margaret. Now, as then, one responded to the
pleasant fantasy, gentle humour and kindly philosophy of this play, but the
questions remained in the mind. What really would happen if we were given
a second chance in life? Suppose, at that crossroads in the lives of all of us,
we had taken the other turning? Barrie's answer is, that nine times out of ten
we would have made the same silly mistakes all over again—but only nine
times out of ten: there remains that tantalising exception to dream about

My first reading of the play in French's Acting edition, had discouraged
me to the point of dismissing it, but by good fortune I was put on the right
road by referring to Ernest Short's excellent "Theatrical Cavalcade".
Apparently it was only after the success of "Quality Street" and "The
Admirable Crichton" that Barrie's plays warranted publication, and for
the book-form he wrote amusing characterisations and stage directions
which might well have been extracts from a full-length novel. Thus the plays
proved as readable as those of Shaw, and came near to representing a new
art-form, midway between novel and play. After reading The Uniform
Edition published by Hodder and Stoughton, the play took on a very
different aspect.

Joy was now seventeen, young for her age and talented, as she would
shortly prove for herself. There was never any doubt that she could win
all hearts as Margaret. There was enough of the seedy Elliston Drury in
Will Dearth to persuade me I could play him, so the real problem lay in
finding Lob, who stands at the very core of the plot, but whose shadowy
character eludes definition. It is from his house on Midsummer's Eve that we
enter the magic wood to be given our second chance. Some go in fun, some
in fear, some in defiance, some in defeat. Lob is, in a mystical sense, one
of the eternals who reveals the souls of mortals. The author says he is small
and "no one has looked so old except a newborn child". He has an air
of portentous gravity, his hands behind his back, his domed head bent, yet
he is so light "that were the ladies to combine, they could blow him out of
his chair". He is much given to little jokes, very agile and vivacious, but
there is an unearthly quality in him which causes his guests to doubt whether
he is the little innocent he would have them believe.

I offered the part to a twenty-eight year old comedian—it must have
been the "domed head" that decided it—and never has there been a luckier
or happier piece of casting. Whenever Bewsey's performance was considered, a single phrase cropped up over and over again; "the spirit of the
play", and he gave it life from the very outset. Bewsey has done much fine
work for us, but I doubt if in artistry he has ever surpassed his portrayal
of Lob.

After that, casting was simple and two characters especially fell delightfully into place. Lob's butler, Matey, "a man of brawn" but a petty

thief with ideas that, but for having taken the wrong turning, he would have been an industrial magnate, was tailor-made for Bob Yaxley. And that being so, Lady Caroline "of the disdainful poise" at whose hands poor Matey must suffer such indignities early in the play, simply had to go to Margery Hall. Remembering their recent exchanges it would be good to see them in the wood as man and wife; he, now the vulgar tycoon, "There's nails in my boots for the ones beneath me," she, mawkishly sentimental, "What fun to write poems about each other and pin them on the trees". Oh, it had to be Marge and Bob!

One who did not grasp the spirit of the play at the outset was Hugh Sawtell. As had become his generous custom, he had my prompt copy interleaved and re-bound; then he read the play and "implored" me (his word) not to do "this impossible stuff". It was typical of Hugh that, sinking his own opinion, he accepted the part of Purdie, a philanderer uncertain to whom next to offer "the devotion of a lifetime", and went on to play it for all he was worth. Before it was all over, a little of the magic had touched Hugh too—but that must remain for him alone.

Of the two ladies currently commanding Purdie's attention, Joanna "the brightest spirit" went to Elizabeth Dyke (type casting again), and Mabel "a safer companion" (h'm, maybe) to Margaret Hulme, making her first appearance with us. Within two years Meg was to become our Secretary and Business Manager, and was destined therefore to take on much of the responsibility and credit for the successful progress of the Players during a difficult period of transition to the status of a properly constituted Society, of which she was later to become Chairman.

For our "older dame" another newcomer closely connected with Foster's School, Mrs. Kathleen Gibling, joined us to play Mrs. Coade, "we call her "Coady"—the nicest". She became "Gibby" to us at once and has always remained so. Gibby was to inspire the choice of our next two plays, "Quiet Wedding" and "Quiet Weekend".

Working at her aunt's Prep. School, "Stonegarth", and deeply interested in drama was Mary Jameson. Providence must have directed us to her, for at the very first reading it was crystal clear that, although young, she was our Alice Dearth, "the darkest spirit, but the bravest". Here was "the spirit of the play" again. Sadly, it was to be Mary's only part with the Players, but those who saw her "Alice" or who worked with her were not quickly to forget her.

That leaves only Mr. Coade "Old, but a sweet pippin of a man". Remembering his "Mr. Pym" of long ago, I thought of Bill Brown and his winning simplicity. Lucky for us, for he not only brought to the part just the right disarming naivete, he did more. He brought his wife with him.

Jessie Brown moved into the prompt corner and there became an institution. I have no idea how many years Jessie remained our prompter, or of the number of plays she monitored for us, but the prompt stool ought certainly to bear an inscription! She was uncannily good at the job, seeming to possess a sixth sense which told her when trouble was looming. Her tiny little voice would always carry to the actor but no further, which is astonishing, because when we "dry" we not only go dumb and daft, but deaf as well. Jessie must have saved many reputations in her day.

The play happily cast, we were now faced with the problem of staging it and to this there was no magical solution. The Church Hall was inevitably in a sorry state and it would take a lot of work by many hands to make it presentable; but worse, the stage had been completely stripped of all its fittings. We retrieved the blue tabs from the Parish Room, but there was no track for them; in short we would have to start again. The Service shows had dealt roughly with our own equipment too, and as we had barely any funds we had to face the fact that we were in no position to present "Dear Brutus" adequately in our old home.

So a decision had to be made which today would be the obvious one, and it must sound a little ridiculous to record that for us it was not easy; for it meant abandoning our first objective. We would, as always, bear our own personal expenses, but for the first time in eleven years a footnote would have to appear in the programme:—

"This Once!
    Profits from the Sherborne performances will be used for the acquisition of much-needed Stage and Lighting Equipment."

In the event, we lost no goodwill; indeed The Western Gazette was very generous about it, stressing that we had already given away over £750 and that "Dear Brutus" was to tour Somerset Schools for various charities. Seymours were generous too: they presented the programmes so that we received the full proceeds.

Once we had made up our minds, there were no half measures. We set out not only to build ambitious sets for our play, but also to meet some basic needs. Thus, for the first time, the Players now acquired a stage-cloth and a sky-cloth. The latter was a rather cumbersome affair, 24ft. wide in all, but the last 4ft. on each side were hinged to fold forward to give a semi-cyc effect. We could now have a couple of powerful F. O. H. spots, for which we were allowed to cut a hatch at the back of the balcony. We could also—a long held ambition—fly the front curtain.

There are only two scenes in "Dear Brutus" but they are not simple. The interior—(Acts I and III)—demands a garden with central flower beds at the back, to change to the edge of a wood during Act I; and in Act III, Lob must be seen asleep in his chair one minute and out tending his flowers the next—without having left the stage! I managed to plot this, together with Act II ("The depths of a wood") quite cleverly I thought, to leave much of the "wood" set standing throughout, and a rather cunning trick exit for

Lob through the fireplace, but when it came to a detailed design I was completely lost. So, once again, off I went to Taunton to see Leonard Meux of the Thespians, who had done "The Scarlet Pimpernel" sets.

As ever, he was kindness itself, dealing gently with my mistakes, but accepting the general idea, and in a week or so I received beautiful scale models which, however, looked much too difficult for us. But no, with John Elliott in charge of woodwork, Diana Wilcoxson and Mrs. Gervis in charge of painting, the empty Methodist School-Room to work in and a new material called Sisalcraft we made the sets between us. Sisalcraft had been much in use as blackout material and looked like two layers of brown paper stuck together with tar. With it we made our first, and only, cyclorama, to back the "wood" scene. (We hoped our fireproofing was effective, but never dared to test it!) Stiffened at intervals with 2 x 1 battens and forming almost a full-semi-circle, it was self-supporting and could be rolled up. Painted darker than the cut-outs and wings, its vague outlines suggested the depths of the wood beyond our little moonlit clearing.

Realising that never more than four characters appeared at once, Len. Meux had fairly filled the stage with slender birches—of blue and white! My secret fears that it might turn out to be a fairy pantomime set were not really banished until Bill Hall finished lighting it to Mr. Meux's plot and Maurie had provided a chemical "night mist" to give life to shafts of moonlight. Our wood scene was not the biggest we have made, but it was the most intricate and we were very proud of it, not only for its dramatic effect but also for its practicability. It could be quickly set and struck and it could be easily toured.

Our production diary reads thus:—
April 26, 27, 28 (mat. & evening) Church Hall, Sherborne.
May
3 Move in at Yeovil—Summerleaze School.
4 Play at Yeovil for R.N. War Libraries.
5 Move back to Church Hall and Play for boys of Sherborne School.
9 Move in at Castle Cary—Ansford Senior School.
10 Play at Castle Cary for "Welcome Home Fund".
11 Move back to Sherborne and rest.
17 Move to Langport—Huish Episcope Senior School.
18 Play at Langport for British Red Cross Society.
19 Move back to Church Hall and Play for Sherborne School for Girls.

Obviously such a programme could not have been contemplated and this chapter in our history could not have been written but for the energy, enthusiasm, ability and the pride of our Stage Staff. "Dear Brutus" marked their ascendancy in our affairs and it may truly be said that for the next two or three years their powerful influence did much in governing all our decisions. And rightly so, for to the Black Gang fell most of the work and a very large slice of the credit for the considerable achievements of the Players during that period.

The team had changed of course. We now had Irwin Crocker and Jim Myers, both future Stage Managers, George Gray, David Lovell, Gerald Brett, young Michael Trevett, (who became assistant electrician and got nick-named "Amburr"), and Mr. and Mrs. Harold Smith. Bunter Fudge was back,—but he had never been away for long. All through his R.A.F. Service he had spent every leave with us, working on the Service Shows. His mother had complained, "He comes home and walks straight up a ladder".

Maurice Welcher was the Stage Director for "Dear Brutus", working the plot, but John Elliott was in charge of the team responsible for building the sets, their transport, the "get-in" and "get out" and shifting and packing during the play. The work was arduous—Castle Cary, for a single example, meant three night stints for the team (but only one for the actors)—it lacked any glamour and it received very little recognition. Yet they liked it and took pride in it, knowing that the show's success was, to a great extent, theirs. Small wonder that as time went by and their effects built our reputation over an ever-widening area, they tended to take the lead, with our actors of secondary importance.

The back-stage hero of them all was dear old Bill Hall, Electrician Extraordinary. With us throughout the war, through all the adventures that followed and on to 1950 when he was Chairman of the Players. W. J. Hall, B.Sc.Tech. was one of the great characters of the early days. Working in often appalling conditions with sparse apparatus he performend absolute wonders for us in the Service shows. It was said of him, unkindly and quite untruthfully, that his first action on arrival was to take out the fuses and replace them with four-inch nails. Once—at Sturminster Newton, when we were faced with no mains supply at all, he covered the floor of the dressing-room with car batteries conjured up from nowhere, and we had light.

Not always in good health, Bill, so far as I can remember, never once let us down. Given normal facilities he was a brilliant stage-electrician, and for me, ideal to work with, for he would grasp the idea I was trying to convey, tell me it was impossible and then get the effect I wanted better than I had visualised it! He was meticulous as to detail; a shadow on the sky was the ruination of the show to him; all stage fittings, standard lamps, table lamps, telephone bells had to be practical; he would rehearse light cues over and over again. Yet, if ever appearances were deceptive! In his pork-pie hat and his Fair Isle pullover stretched a bit tight round his middle, surrounded by an apparently inextricable tangle of wire perilously twisted together, he resembled nothing so much as a rather tubby, outraged cherub, exasperated beyond endurance. There was never enough time, the plugs wouldn't fit, he must have more space. "Quite impossible—out of the question". "Fred, do you understand? Are you listening Fred? It—can—not—be—done." Yet, in all the years, on all the stages we worked together, I cannot remember a missed lighting cue.

It is the lot of the stage eletrician to be noticed only when things go wrong. His major contribution to the dramatic impact of the play, his carefully applied skill in conveying the time of day, the state of the weather, the season of the year; his cunning illusion that the little pool of light from that single table-lamp really comes only from the lamp—it all goes unrecognised; understandably, by the audience, less so, all too often, by the actors. And as for the Press, he will be fortunate to find his name at the tail-end of the also rans. Bill Hall, however, was getting noticed. He had already received congratulations on his work in "I Killed The Count"—"Clever lighting effects in the difficult flash-back sequences". Now, in "Dear Brutus" he really came into his own, sharing top honours with Len Meux. "The depths of a wood in the enchantment of a Moonlit night" was in truth a triumph for them. Never have we, the actors owed more to the technicians than here, in creating the atmosphere essential to this delicate piece of fantasy.

None of us, Bill least of all, could have guessed, however, what powers of enchantment were possessed by Lob's mysterious wood itself, once it appeared. Some of its wonders were not to be seen just yet, but it can now be recorded in all seriousness that of those Players who entered the wood, two never came out again. Margery Hall, 38 (Spinster and Company Director) and Robert Yaxley, 52 (Royal Navy) fell deeply and wonderfully in love. The precious relationship which Lady Caroline and Matey found in the wood was to unite them for the rest of their days, for here were two souls who truly took "the right turning".

At first, like that other couple, from "A Midsummer Night's Dream", the course of their true love ran not smooth and, like them, they were parted for a while. But came the day in 1946 when Doris (stronger again now and able to help with props in "Dear Brutus") and Margery went to London together, but Doris came home alone. Margery returned somewhat later, all aglow and wearing the most ridiculous hat; and she and Bob were married that summer.

They settled in a charming little weather-boarded house on the village green of a Kentish beauty spot and it was there that they greeted Doris and me thirteen years later, when I went to manage Lloyds at Ashford. Later still—I was alone then—this happy pair proved good friends indeed to me and we spent many pleasant hours together. There were evenings with them at the Ellen Terry Memorial Theatre at Smallhythe for Celebrity visits —Sybil Thorndyke was one—and there in 1964 I saw Bob acting again— as Philostrate in a very high-brow "Dream". Sitting in the audience with his fond proud wife, I remembering thinking how aptly their "wood" scene was still being acted out in their life together after nearly twenty years.

Cynics will laugh it all off no doubt and maintain that this serene marriage would have come about in any case, but before the magic of Lob's mysterious wood is dismissed too lightly, the scoffers should bear in mind that "Dear Brutus" led us to our greatest adventure of all, one beyond our wildest dreams; that it brought to us all an experience never forgotten and that for me it made a dream come true with such authenticity and realism that it can only be thought of as a revelation. "Dear Brutus" had, for us, a mystical, magical quality of its own. So let them scoff.

Even the Philistines would admit that our 1945 production of the play served us uncommonly well on a material level. The tour made about £100 for the various causes, and from the six Sherborne performances we became rich. For the first time we had £109 in the Bank, and that after purchasing equipment costing £131 and spending more on the Church Hall.

Sticking rigidly to my old ideas, I am on record as disapproving of the money in the Bank, which exposes me as the bigot I must have been, and it underlines the fact that I was in fact, beginning to become committee-ridden.

As Secretary and Business Manager, Margery and, in her turn, Meg Hulme had one drawback in common. They were both much too given to holding Committee Meetings! and in this, I am sorry to say, they had the backing of Brookie who was playing an increasing role in our affairs as Treasurer, and of W. J. Cordy who always seemed to find himself Chairman (unappointed). So now instead of just getting on with the business of play production, everything had to be proposed and seconded, minuted and approved. And as we always seemed to pass everything unanimously it all appeared to me a terrible waste of time,—besides, I didn't like having my wings clipped. No doubt it was all for our eventual good, but there it is; I hate committees!

A footnote—"The Dear Brutus" tour of Somerset Schools was noticed in the Bristol papers—John Bennett still going on about "It's Autumn Now" six years earlier and our link with Bristol Wartime Entertainers—and this was to have considerable bearing on our future. We welcomed the wider publicity, but had little idea where it was to lead us.

THE BLACKMORE VALE DANCE ORCHESTRA 1928

THE SHERBORNE AMATEUR OPERATIC AND DRAMATIC SOCIETY

PRESENT

"THE MIKADO"

or "THE TOWN OF TITIPU"

(by permission of R. D'Oyly Carte, Esq.)

by W. S. Gilbert and Arthur Sullivan.

DRAMATIS PERSONÆ :

The Mikado of Japan	Richmond McIntosh
Nanki-Poo (his son, disguised as a wandering minstrel, and in love with Yum-Yum)	Vernon House
Ko-Ko (Lord High Executioner of Titipu)	Fred. B. Alcock
Pooh-Bah (Lord High Everything Else)	Hugh Elder
Pish-Tush (a noble Lord)	Frederick Gillard
Yum-Yum .. ⎰ Three sisters ⎱	Marjorie Lowman
Pitti-Sing .. ⎱ (wards of ⎰	Rosemary James
Peep-Bo .. ⎰ Ko-Ko) ⎱	Dulcie Hunt
Katisha (an elderly lady, in love with Nanki-Poo)	Mrs. Ernest Hodgson

CHORUS.

School Girls.

Mesdames J. M. Brown, L. Cleverley, M. Diblee, A. Freeman, M. Harkins, W. Hewson, J. Hutton, M. Hall, E. Morris, E. Otton, J. Parry-Jones, A. Shepherd, I. Shaw, D. Stephens, M. Wardlaw, M. Warr, E. Young. N. Young, D. Young.

Nobles.

Messrs. W. J. E. Brown, H. Dodge, D. B. Eperson, G. W. Fox, C. A. Lowman, G. Lowman, C. Pettitt, J. H. Randolph, D. Stewart, P. J. Shaw, A. R. Trevett, W. L. Warr.

Guards.

Messrs. H. Pitman, H. D. Trevett.

Coolies.

Masters G. D. Batchelor, R. Pedley.

Attendant.

Master David Hunt.

ACT 1. Courtyard of Ko-Ko's Official Residence.

ACT 2. Ko-Ko's Garden.

The Opera is produced under the personal supervision of Dr. Richmond McIntosh.

Costumes and Scenery :—By B. J. SIMMONS AND CO., LTD., LONDON.

Business Manager	MR. ROWLAND REEVES.
Property Master ..	MR. K. DIBBLE.
Wardrobe Mistress	MISS G. PINECOFFIN.
Stage Manager	MR. S. S. WALLER.
Electrician	MR. J. DOOTSON (*D.C. Electric Co.*)
Dancing Instructress ..	MISS DOROTHY THOMPSON.
Accompanist	MR. C. L. P. HUTCHINGS.
Perruquier	MR. W. L. WARR.

"TONS OF MONEY"
above—Peggy Merrick

below—Muriel Davis and W. J. Cardy speak the opening lines of The Players' first production

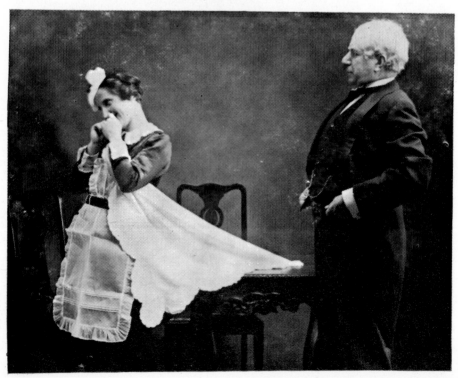

"NO
NO
NANETTE"

Pat and Betty Shaw

Joan Waller, Betty Shaw, Eileen Wright, Peggy Henstridge,
Sybil Epton, Beryl Chaffin, Ethel Seeley, Beryl Heath

above—Pat Shaw and "the Bachelors"

l-r: Ross Biles, Bill Vaux, Bob Hazzard, George Elliott, Ralph Hamblin, George Philpott, Joey Brown

below—Jack Perham and "the Maids"

ALF. COLLINGS

Landlord of the Mermaid Hotel.
The Players' first home

"NIGHT MUST FALL"

DAN

W. J. Cordy
(Lord Chief Justice)

Winifred Hickson
(Olivia)

l-r: Winifred Hickson, Eva Gillam, Doris Alcock, F.B.A., T. Elms Dyke

"THE SCARLET PIMPERNEL"

Act 1   Scene 1

"WARTIME . . . —VARIETY"

Some of the Regulars

Wilby Shaw

Bewsey Dyke

Bill Brown and Jessie

Mavis Gigg

"Chaff"

Mervyn G. Davies

Geoffrey Scalbert

Some of the Black Gang
Ken Blackmore, Bill Hall,
George Philpott, Bunter Fudge

Mrs. Harold Smith's
"JUVENILE PLAYERS OF SHERBORNE"
(Polly's Pantos)

"I KILLED THE COUNT"

above—Bewsey Dyke and Gerald Brett

below—M. M. Welcher, George Gray and B. R. Yaxley, R.N.

"DEAR BRUTUS"

standing: W. J. E. Brown, A. Hugh Sawtell, Mary Jameson
Seated: Margery Hall, Kathleen G bling
Kneeling: Elizabeth Dyke, Bewsey B. Dyke, Margaret Hulme

l-r: W. J. E. Brown, Elizabeth Dyke, Margery Hall, B. R. Yaxley

THEATRE ROYAL, BRISTOL

"SPRING 1600"

Joy Alcock
as
Anne Byrd/Jack Beeston

"SPRING 1600"

above—P. R. Daudney, Jim Saunders
l-r: Cyril Copp, Joy Alcock, Kathleen Gibling

below—Ernest Hulme as Richard Burbage with his company

CHAPTER SEVENTEEN

FROM THE OUTSIDE

At a meeting at Seyco House on the 25th July 1945 it was proposed, seconded and passed unanimously that we would produce "Quiet Wedding" in aid of Coombe Church Organ Fund. At this point I resigned. As I had never been appointed to anything I must have looked rather silly, and so did the reason I put forward.

The "committee"—also unappointed—at this time were Cordy, Brooks, Welcher, Sawtell, Hall, Elliott, Alcock and the Secretary, Miss Hall; and they all made appropriate noises in protest, except one. To my private consternation, my boss, Brookie expressed the view that an alternative Director should be sought who would be prepared to take over production if called upon.

I failed completely to grasp what was in Brookie's mind, for I knew nothing then of his hopes and endeavours for my future. I had given it very little thought myself, and vaguely expected to remain Chief Clerk at Lloyds, Sherborne for the rest of my days. So I sat silent and rather unhappy whilst it was decided to ask Gerald Brett to undertake the Autumn Production, and the meeting passed on to "other business". This consisted mostly of confirming transactions already concluded, such as renting part of the old Baptist Chapel in Trendle Street—the Tin Tabernacle—from Mr. Bow for our scenery and equipment at 5/- a week which I had, it seems, arranged without authority, and the more weighty decisions I had come to with Mr. Steele about expenditure at the Church Hall.

Now that we were people of property, with assets and money in the Bank, I could understand that the Players ought to have some sort of corporate being, but we were moving too far away from the original concept for my peace of mind. (I said at the start that I could not defend the concept; I have since admitted to an unreasonable adherence to my own views and my inability to recognise changing circumstances.) Thus, whilst I was quite happy to have my decisions confirmed by the Players' Officers if that pleased them, I did not intend to submit my ideas for discussion and amendment, dithering and delay. At this time, for instance, I was keen to bring C.E.M.A. plays to Sherborne (Council for the Encouragement of Music and Arts—forerunner of the Arts Council) with the Players sponsoring and providing facilities, but unwisely I mentioned the idea in committee, and so many objections and doubts were raised that it died and the C.E.M.A. companies visited Yeovil instead.

No, I would have to keep my ideas to myself and, if necessary, go ahead by myself, as in 1934; and there was one particularly exciting possibility keeping me awake at night just then, an idea which certainly would never have got off the ground had I submitted it to a committee for discussion.

My resignation did not amount to much. Gerald commenced work on "Quiet Wedding" and it was going well when he fell ill. Eventually he decided he would have to stand down and I found myself holding the book once again. It entailed a week's delay in production date but in general I was able to go on from where he left off and, judging from the reception, it went well.

Audiences were welcomed in a freshly painted Church Hall furnished with much better seating than ever before; there was even a "Cloaks" with attendant. On stage, our new counter-weight system lifted the Curtain smoothly and we could "drop-in" the little inset Act II Scene II complete, a scene change in under one minute.

All this in the spirit of mutual trust and co-operation existing between the Trustees and the Players ever since 1938; all agreed between us in a brief chat every so often with Mr. Steele in his shop in Cheap Street. I had a very great respect and liking for him personally and I was grateful for the frank and informal way in which we could discuss business. From all our performances now we were making some contribution to improvements in addition to the rent, and I promised that in 1946 we would devote the full proceeds of a production to the Church Hall Funds. In return, whilst we had to remember the multi-purpose use of the Hall, we could have matters more or less our own way.

Years later, and many miles away, I still used to day-dream of what we might have done with it between us.

*   *   *   *   *

Esther McCracken's comedy "Quiet Wedding" first appeared in 1938, and our audiences greeted it now with fond nostalgia for "life as it used to be before the War". Much, much later, 1965-72 there was to be considerable professional interest in revivals of the play as a period piece which amusingly reflected middle-class life in the late thirties, and it enjoyed quite a success all over again then.

For us, the central character, which in London Marjorie Fielding had made so much her own, was in the safe hands of Gibby (Mrs. Gibling), but she didn't keep the honours to herself. Gerald's wife, Phyllis Brett had joined us to play Aunt Mary with an air of quiet, kindly wisdom which endeared her to us all. Phyl Shelton (nee Brett) joined us also, to play Bella ("Waiting at the Church"). Those two are still greeted as Mary and Bella to this day. Joy got the chance to grow up, and made the most of it, in a comedy role—a good exercise for her; but by far the biggest laughs of the play were earned quite unintentionally by Polly Smith as Aunt Florence. Her telephone conversation was the funniest thing in the show and Polly still doesn't know why they laughed. Unwittingly she gave us all a lesson on the importance to any comedian of being absurd seriously.

At the end of it all we had given £142 to Coombe Church, £40 to the Church Hall and, from an extra performance, £34 to Gt. Ormond Street Hospital for Children. A success certainly, but one from which I felt slightly apart, as if I had come in from outside half-way through to help out.

And the truth of that is my thoughts just then were elsewhere.

CHAPTER EIGHTEEN

THEATRE ROYAL

I thought the letter would never come. Not that I expected much from it when it did, for my rather pushing suggestion had invited a polite rebuff at best.

It must have been six weeks—perhaps two months—since I had read in the evening paper of the plans for the Bristol Guild of Players' Full-length Play Festival to be staged at The Theatre Royal for a week in April 1946. The columnist had suggested that in view of the prestige attached to filling the bill at The Royal the net should be cast wider and the Festival thrown open so that the six companies finally invited to appear would represent "the Best in the West".

My little letter of tentative enquiry to John Bennett brought a quick and encouraging response. If I cared to write to the Guild Secretary, Miss Barbara Rogers, giving a full history of our accomplishments and seeking selection he would support me. He hoped his own Thirteen Players would be appearing.

Although I was proud of all we had done, it didn't look much on paper and I made many attempts before I finally got the letter off, saying that if invited we would be happy to present "Dear Brutus" as the Festival. A brief and distant little acknowledgement told me I would be advised in due course, and encouraged me not at all.

The Bristol Guild of Players were new to me, but The Theatre Royal had been in the news in recent years—since 1942, in fact, when a public appeal had been launched to save "this amazing rarity" as Mr. Robert Donat put it, "the history theatre par exellence". C.E.M.A. had then leased the building and The Theatre Royal became the first State Theatre in the Country. After spending £8,000 on repairs (in war-time too) the theatre re-opened in May 1943 with "She Stoops to Conquer" (Dame Sybil Thorndyke as Mrs. Hardcastle). Now, in 1946 the Arts Council had arranged with the London Old Vic to place a residential company in Bristol and a splendid new era opened, equalling, perhaps surpassing, anything in the Royal's previous history. The number of Bristol Old Vic productions which have transferred to the West End with great critical acclaim and financial success says all there is to say. The outstanding example is perhaps "Salad Days" which, after Bristol, had a record London run of 2,283 performances.

My personal experience of the Royal had been confined to the early twenties when its affairs were at a low ebb. Then, a bald head in the pit was a sure target for orange peel and toffee papers from above. Its entertainment was such as to attract us youths, I am sorry to admit, on reprehensible escapades. No respect then, on nights out from Bath, for the theatre's illustrious, if chequered history, no heed that we were playing the fool in a place now almost revered by theatre lovers. For Bristol Theatre Royal is the oldest theatre in England in continuous use as a theatre, and its association with great actors and actresses of the past gives it a position unequalled among provincial playhouses.

In 1766, it needed courage to open a theatre within the City boundary and in the area covered by its magistrates. The proposal faced fierce opposition from the clergy and City authorities, and it was accused in print of "ruining the morals of our youth, impoverishing our tradesmen, promoting the arts of intrigue and of seducing the innocent, diffusing a habit of idleness, indolence and debauchery". Well, I can testify that in 1923 some at least of those fears may have been justified! But not, it seems, in 1766, for this was at the height of the success and sophistication of Bristol's merchant class, and enough local men of substance came forward to provide the project with finance and an aura of respectability.

The first performance in the new theatre took place on 30th May, 1766 with a prologue written by Garrick, but to avoid liability to prosecution it was advertised as "a Concert of Music and a specimen of 'Rhetorick' ". The theatre did not become legalised until 1778 when King George III's Royal Licence was granted, and from then until 1817 it enjoyed some of its most prosperous years, linked to the Bath Theatre Royal Company who also performed in Bristol. During this period every English actor of note played there, Sarah Siddons, her sister Frances, the Edwins, William Charles Macready (whose family managed the theatre for some years) and many others. By 1860 the Royal was admitted to be the finest school for actors in the country. Mrs. Kendall, Mrs. Bancroft, Kate and Ellen Terry were all trained there.

Now, from 1946 onwards, history is repeating itself for the Theatre Royal; its early glories have been restored to it and the bad times (following the opening of the new Princes in more fashionable Park Row) may be forgotten; unless it is to recall that even then, at the very worst, it always remained a theatre, never put to any other use. When it did close for short periods it was because the bailiffs were in or the tenant out. If there is one place in the whole world where an amateur might sense for a moment what the theatre is really all about, it must be here; and even the remotest possibility that the Players might stage a full production on this historic stage was enough to fire the imagination and keep me in suspense for weeks.

When, at last, the invitation came it was so late in the day as to lead me to suspect we had only been accepted as a substitute for some Bristol casualty. Of the six to appear we were the only company to come from outside the City, so either the idea of spreading the net had not found favour or the "Best in the West" were all in Bristol! Fair enough, for it was a Guild Festival and they had more than fifty affiliated groups, all Bristolians. We were wonderfully lucky to be invited, albeit as a second choice and the lone outsider; and I suspect we owed much to John Bennett's influence.

Once in, we were warmly welcomed. All sorts of help could be laid on if required and Barbara Rogers responded eagerly to all my queries and requests. The only possible doubt about the adventure was financial, for although we ought to do well on our percentage, the Guild guarantee was as low as £15. But this was no time for qualms, the prospect was too exciting. So Margery had to be steered away from calling committee meetings and all efforts directed to getting "Dear Brutus", complete and self-contained to Bristol in about four weeks.

Marge and Bob had been parted at this juncture, so we now lacked a Matey, but back from the war came Ernest Hulme to take over. Otherwise the cast was intact and the play came to life again smoothly and with renewed pleasure for us all.

Scenery, however, was a problem. The interior could be built up to the necessary 14 feet, but the "wood" had to be remade and timber was unobtainable. The situation called for ingenuity and the kind of luck which always seemed to come the way of "Dear Brutus". Hence the story of Crocker and The Tree.

Irwin Crocker had for many years been chauffeur and factotum to Dr. Rickett, but he was now working for George Spiller, and it was whilst out making deliveries that he saw The Tree at Newell House. Jack Lugg tells me it was the biggest Poplar in Dorset with a trunk forty-five feet in circumference and stood higher than any other in Sherborne. But it was not standing at all when Crocker saw it, it was down, obstructing the road, and had to be moved quickly. Some of it went to Lugg and Copp, some to the Castle yard and from each of those, some, within four weeks, on to the stage of the Theatre Royal, Bristol.

Crock had joined our Black Gang twelve months earlier when we were building the first D.B. sets in the cold, dirty, disused Wesleyan Schoolroom in Abbey Road. Amongst his Home Guard comrades he had gained quite a name for finding otherwise unobtainable snacks for those on guard, and it was one such good turn which brought him to see us one winter's night with tit-bits from Coombs Restaurant—only to find a paint-brush in his hand.

He got the idea from the very start. A good handyman, he worked with tremendous enthusiasm and no thought for himself. Now, with two shows and a tour behind him he was experienced in our ways, as keen as ever and to the fore in all our stagework. Not the least of his attributes was his remarkable gift for finding the unobtainable, but even this deserted him in the depressing search for timber. He tried his old Home Guard pals, Cecil Eason and Jack Lugg but they, like everyone else, could offer all the help needed, but no wood.

Then, across the road from Easons he saw the tree! A few questions and up to the Castle Yard where he told the foreman the most heart-rending story of Sherborne's pride in the Players' appearance before a celebrated audience in Bristol, and all in ruins for the want of a few bits of wood. Well, we got all the 3in. x 1in. we needed for our new woodland set; it was green and wet, and it whipped in all directions, but it stood up. From Lugg and Copp came a beautifully shaped set of steps from the same tree, all free and for nothing.

Details of the Festival sent to us had included a stage plan but we decided to go and see for ourselves. So, one day quite early on, a few of us, Bill Hall (with that great rarity, a bottle of whisky for Mr. Hickson, Manager of The Royal), Crock, Margery and I sat through a matinee of "The Beaux Stratagem" with Pamela Brown and William Devlin (the opening production of the new Bristol Old Vic Company) and then introduced ourselves.

We were made to feel welcome, were shown all round and met the stage carpenter and the electrician with whom we would be corresponding over scene and lighting plots. Mr. Hickson took me up into the roof space above the ceiling of the auditorium to see the famous "thunder-run", a sequence of wooden troughs down which were rolled cannon balls to give a most effective imitation of thunder overhead. He also took me under the stage to see the (mostly) Victorian machinery, lifts, traps counter-balanced platforms.

Only when I trod on the stage itself did my sense of wonder and excitement evaporate, for here was something we had never had to cope with—a very steep rake. Not only would there be problems in erecting the sets, but the actors would find it most disconcerting. We were certainly going to experience the true meaning of "up stage" and "downstage"! There could not have been many such stages left in 1946, and that one has gone now. As part of the extensive alterations made during the Sixties the theatre now has a new fly-tower and a flat stage.

We were to have the honour of playing on the final night of the Festival and were guaranteed not only a full house but a distinguished audience, for it was to be something of an occasion. The new Arts Council of Great Britain and the Trustees of the Theatre Royal were to be represented at high level, and members of Theatre Guilds were coming from London, Southampton, Cardiff and Swindon for the Saturday performance.

The Thirteen Players were to open the Festival in "Berkeley Square", followed by "Mourning Becomes Electra" (Part One), Lennox Robinson's "The White-headed Boy", "A Bill of Divorcement" (Clemence Dane), Ibsen's "Hedda Gabler", and "Dear Brutus".

The Adjudicator, John Bourne, was the best-known in the Country. Editor of "Amateur Theatre" and "Theatrecraft", he had been on the editorial staff of "The Times" and had written dramatic criticism for "The Observer": Author of the only text-book on "Drama Festivals" he had himself adjudicated thousands of plays. He was an acknowledged authority on the acting of Shakespeare and Ibsen. John Bourne's reputation was such that he was held in some awe by all whose work was submitted for his assessment.

Having obtained a block of 60 dress circle seats, Margery booked rooms at the Grand Hotel for the company and we returned to Sherborne with a considerable sense of occasion. April 6th was going to be an important date for us.

Most of our time now was concerned with the mechanics of assembly, transport and mounting the show rather than with interpretation of the play, and this may have helped, for we did know the play very well and might have got stale. There were detailed scene and lighting plots to be despatched in advance, (in this instance I asked for the moon and got it!). Properties to be found again (back to Meredith Thomas for his palette, brushes and easel and the picture of the wood he had painted for me) and some extra scenery to build (our little cyc. would not do—it had to be The Royal's sky-cloth with a new "dense" cut-out). The new Wessex Club lent us a large carpet, and their shield depicting the Wessex Wyvern which we proudly displayed as part of the decor. Everyone appeared to want help in some way. The extent of public interest was surprising—and very heartening. Our 60 tickets could have been sold over and over again, and we took it as a great compliment to learn that the audience would include Gen. R. L. Waller, Chairman of Sherborne U.D.C. and Mr. E. J. Freeman, Clerk.

I kept one little bit of preparation to myself, as a surprise for the company on the night. I obtained the band parts of "Summer Days" and sent them on to Bristol Light Orchestra, who were to be in the pit throughout the week, with detailed instructions and the hope expressed that I could have a word with the conductor before the show.

Hugh Sawtell had a much better surprise for us though. Privately he produced a magnificent Souvenir Programme for presentation to everyone connected with the show. Of highest quality, it must have cost a great deal. Its semi-stiff cover was printed in blue, silver and black for our crest (in keeping with the woodland scene) and it contained reproductions of the stage photographs from 1945. Many examples of Hugh's great generosity to the Players passed unknown to most of us, I fear, and so were never acknowledged, but this was a gift treasured by each one of us all through the years as a delightful memento of our greatest adventure, and today, thirty years later, it still brings back the thrills of that night for us all.

Our scenery, furniture and props despatched in a hired furniture van, we set out on Friday in time to settle in at the hotel and walk round to the theatre. A few got there in time to see "Hedda Gabler", and of these Hugh came out in the interval, having had enough! The others brought back terrifying accounts of the insensitive reactions of the audience, the laughter in all the wrong places, and the general restlessness. In due course, John Bourne dealt very severely with this behaviour, I was told, for he found much to praise in this performance of his favourite Ibsen play. But this was no comfort to me; if Joy and I were to be treated like that by an audience I knew we would both curl up; and we were vulnerable. We had from the start taken care to bowl the father and daughter scene along briskly, getting the fun out of it, never allowing sentiment to become sentimentality. Nevertheless, it contained patches of dangerously thin ice where the sympathy of our audience was vital. I was scared.

Next day, the stage was ours from 10 a.m. and I think the butterflies were pretty active in all of us as we turned into the little alleyway behind the theatre, but from the moment we found our scenery and props, all neatly packed in the scene dock, all was well. The slow, sure, flat-footed way in which the professional stage staff dealt with each little problem in turn did wonders for our confidence. Unhurriedly our woodland scene went up first and only then, when it was fully set, did the Theatre Electrician appear.

Ernest Peppin was elderly and, with the Stage Carpenter, virtually lived in the theatre, working, they claimed, seventy hours a week. Inclined to be taciturn at first and disdainful of the amateurish lighting plot I had sent him, he stood silent out on the apron for a minute, looking over the set. One question about the "moonbeam", and then, "Go away and leave me alone with it for an hour. Bert, I'll want the Pageant". We went.

It was an instructive hour, spent in sorting out dressing rooms (I was going to dress in MacCready's room!) and getting the "feel" of the theatre. It was then we first learned of the quite serious betting on the result of the Festival, a most reprehensible practice, much frowned upon, but rather fun if one is not a punter but merely a runner. Regarded as country cousins, we had been at long odds to start with, but following some severe drubbings early in the week and the fact that we were bringing a fully "self-contained" production which had already toured successfully, we were lying fourth on Saturday morning. Favourite by a long way was the Lennox Robinson comedy "The White Headed Boy" which had played on Wednesday to an enthusiastic reception.

The best remembered character we met in finding our way around was the Fireman, who addressed us very severely on the subject of fire precautions and the rigid "no smoking" rules to be observed. He gave us a vivid account of how he had saved the theatre from destruction during the war by hurling incendiaries off the roof (quite true, too, I believe) but I found it difficult to take my eyes off the cigarette in his mouth. Apparently he was the only man allowed to smoke back-stage!

We were told later that Ernie Peppin had not displayed so much interest all the week as he was now showing, and when an excited Bill Hall led us out to see our woodland set from the front, the result had me gasping my thanks to him. Crock had just got his "electro-chemical" mist enveloping the trees and from high up in the O.P. wing a huge, old-fashioned but wonderfully effective "Pageant" spot shed a soft moonbeam on to the main acting area. The scene had been given a wonderful atmosphere of depth and mystery, such as we could never have achieved on our own. Len Meux, the designer, would have seen his vision fulfilled and more; I wish he had been with us just then.

With Peppin now warmly on our side, we set the interior and lit it before lunch. Ernie and Bill got on well together and the lighting cues all worked quite smoothly. So now it was up to the actors.

We had to rehearse during the afternoon rather longer than I had hoped, for we not only had to accustom ourselves to the alarming rake on the stage but to playing into a battery of F.O.H. spots and to an audience many of whom were high above us. It was the first time we had ever had to "play to the Gods" and we found it strange. Doris and Bunter, from the back of the gallery, were quite severe in admonishment—they could not hear and only saw the tops of our heads—so we had to aim higher. The practice was well worthwhile.

Just as we were finishing, a happy coincidence; the conductor of the orchestra called in with his pianist, so instead of the hoped-for chat, we could actually time the music cues with the curtains and end-of-play action. Then back to the Grand to lie down until 7 o'clock.

I remember all this very clearly, but of the performance, not much in detail. I do recall the excitement of the house filling up and the orchestra tuning as I went through my usual futile routine of fidgeting nervously with the furniture on the set, moving a chair a few inches, moving it again and eventually leaving it where it had been originally. I do remember the thrill of "Summer Days" coming from the pit, the tiny swish as the curtain rose and then the expectant hush of a packed house. Theatre Royal—the real thing!

The rest is remembered only as a dream come true, an experience beyond my power to describe objectively. I believe the performance was good. I would certainly have remembered had there been any bad moments. Our new Matey did wonders to steady a slightly nervous opening by the five ladies—Ernest, firm as a rock, as ever. Mary Jamieson skilfully negotiated one of the thinnest patches of ice, in her scene as a vagrant woman, whimpering; (but "here and there ragged graces still cling and unruly passion smoulders"). The author's instructions here set Mary the most difficult piece in the play in which to avoid slipping into bathos, but it was accepted with sympathy and respect and we knew we were not to suffer as "Hedda Gabler" had done the night before.

There are more hazy impressions of a happy, satisfying performance generously received; but for me, understandably I hope, memory comes clearly into focus only in a close-up of the scene with Joy.

Occupying rather more than half the second act, this brief encounter between a transformed Dearth and his "dream" daughter gave me on this night probably the most intense personal experience of my life. Never before or since has there been anything quite like it. It was much more for me than a dream come true, for those twenty minutes or so brought the realisation of all my hopes, day-dreams, aspirations—and regrets—accumulated from early boyhood. Here, in actual experience, I was getting my "second chance", knowing in real life what "might have been". If it is I who am now guilty of bathos, forgive please and understand, for that is how it must remain. Here I was, on the stage of the oldest professional theatre in England, playing to a sophisticated and highly critical audience the finest "Father and Daughter" scene ever written for the English stage—with my own daughter. My daughter Joy, moreover, with an inborn talent, a budding technique, a capacity for conscientious work amounting to dedication and a winsome unaffected style, whose "Margaret" tonight would have graced the professional stage. It is, of course, a "doting daddy" who says so but, let it be remembered, events were to prove me right, and before very long.

Although now eighteen, Joy had no difficulty in shedding the few years needed for "Margaret" and the experience she had gained in the twelve months since she had first essayed the part brought her confidence and some expertise. Now from within her deeply felt portrayal she had learnt to gauge audience reaction and tonight we could "bounce" the scene forward together happily, actually feeling the warmth of the response.

Maintaining the pace, pointing the fun and gaiety and the affectionate raillery in the exchanges, Joy cleverly avoided any hint of embarrassment in the tender moments, when, for instance, Margaret made her well-loved Dad shut his eyes while she put her hair up for the very first time, using a little woodland pool as a mirror, and then allowed him a glimpse of the Margaret to be. It could so easily have become sloppily sentimental, but not in Joy's hands.

By the time her little piece of childhood nonsense in balancing a biscuit on her nose and catching it in her mouth like a puppy had drawn a spontaneous and unexpected round of applause, I knew she had won them. Yet, through all the youthful high spirits and light-hearted banter, she had succeeded in conveying, exactly as the author intended, the reality and permanence of the precious bond uniting this father and daughter. It was success in this which built up for her the tragic atmosphere and moving appeal of the scene's final moments, the climax of the whole play.

It lives most vividly in the memory. Margaret, alone in the wood now, and suddenly frail, bravely counting up to a hundred against the return of her father, her voice faltering and frightened as the wood darkened around her, the moon overclouded; her stumbling little run from tree to tree and finally the choking, small cry as she grasped that it had not been real at all, that she was only a "might have been". She was almost lost to sight as the curtain came gently down, and in the darkness the silence held. Alone upon the stage of this historic theatre my eighteen year old daugher held a packed house captivated. Joy finished with tears in her eyes, but not for a moment had she lost control either of herself or her audience.

The second act reception affected us all. The dressing-rooms, hitherto more subdued than ever before, became animated and carefree. Crock dashed in to tell us we were now joint favourites to win—and I got a bad attack of "last act nerves". So often things go wrong or the show gets ragged at the end. In my own experience there had hardly ever been a last night absolutely free of trouble, and it usually comes in the last scene. (In "Iolanthe" I had actually left it until my bit in the very last chorus on the last night to make a silly mistake). For years and years I have begged actors not to lose their first-night edge until after the last night's final curtain, and never more earnestly than on this night.

I need not have feared, for tonight every one of us found a little something extra and together we carried the play crisply through to an effective close. For once, and it has been a very rare experience, as the curtain came down I felt a sense of complete satisfaction, for we could not have bettered this performance within our limited ability, and I knew it,

There was still one more moment to remember. After our first line-up (without the "dream-daughter") we took carefully rehearsed individual calls, Hugh with Meg Hulme and Liz Dyke, Bill Brown and Gibby, Ernest and Marge, Mary and I. Then, last but one, Lob materialised magically from the depths of his arm-chair (a terrific reception for Bewsey) crossed and turned at the exit to crook a finger beckoning Margaret into the room for the first time.

And that is what I can still see now when I close my eyes. The slight little figure of Joy standing shyly far upstage, the quite rapturous applause engulfing her, the formal little curtsy and, as it still went on, the bowed head. I had never, never felt so proud and happy—until the idiot started to move for the exit before the curtain was down. It won us another line-up though, and we had the great pleasure of seeing John Bourne and the officials having to wait in the wings until we were allowed to go. If audience response was anything to go by, we must have done well.

But it wasn't. Those who had backed us at short odds must have had some nasty moments, for apparently John Bourne declared an interest at the very start, admitting to a strong dislike for the plays of J. M. Barrie "and all that whimsy". Amusingly he recounted the number of times he had been compelled to sit through the sickly sentimentality of the father and daughter scene; but he does not seem to have raised much of a laugh and it transpired that he was in fact leading up to a very pretty compliment to us.

I was told all that later, for I missed the introductory speeches and Mr. Bourne's opening remarks. For me it was all over; anything now was an anti-climax and with my head in the clouds following our reception on this night of all, I was not in a frame of mind to take disparaging comments, however helpful. So I went back to the dressing-room to take off my make-up, tidy up and get back into my dinner jacket—if only I could find it. That in turn meant finding a rather tubby young admirer of Joys, a King's School boy who had somehow managed to get back-stage and had appointed himself my dresser. That is to say he had helped me with the quick change into my artist's garb in the wings at the very end of the play; since when he had disappeared with my dinner jacket and probably my daughter too.

But no. I found all three in the wings, Joy biting her fingernails to the quick as she hung on Mr. Bourne's words. So now I could go properly dressed to accept the Guild of Players trophy; for there was no shadow of doubt in my mind as to the result, such was my sense of euphoria. Had I known the markings so far, I should have come down to earth with a bump; "Hedda Gabler" had been awarded 90%—so much for audience response!

Mr. Bourne was getting down to detail:—A very good evening, with music and well-controlled lighting . . . Plenty of atmosphere in the wood scene, which was acted with charm . . . The production showed a mind behind it that sought out the essence . . . Movements had meaning . . . groupings successful . . . good timing and flowing dialogue. We all received little compliments:—Lob, in the true spirit of fantasy without overdoing it . . . Margaret, a tender and lovable study . . . Dearth, an artist . . . Matey, "I liked him enormously" and so on. Finally:—"Almost free from any criticism, which testifies to the high all-round standard achieved and pays tribute to the work of the producer."

At last the summary. None of the plays Mr. Bourne had seen had been awarded less than 75 marks, and the highest went to Amateur Players of Sherborne with 92.

I should have been deeply ashamed of my presumption, for I had not realised just how much it meant to me to be there, nervous and trembling, to be presented with the trophy by Mr. Wilfred Leighton, Chairman of the Theatre Royal Trustees, and it was all rather overwhelming. The whole house seemd to be erupting around me, from out front, high above and back-stage too. I managed to stumble through a little speech of thanks, down came the curtain, and it was all congratulations and back-slapping and photographs.

The party as the Grand went on until late. The Guild Chairman, Mr. Scott-Piggot and Barbara Rogers brought Mr. Bourne over, and there were some from competing companies, all very generous and jolly. But we were so tired.

Nor was it the only celebration. Crocker had phoned the news back to the Wessex Club in Sherborne and glasses were raised there. Moreover the coach-load of supporters plus a small fleet of cars broke their journey home just outside Bristol for a meal which became quite a party and it was here (I believe Brookie and Elsie Coombs were at the bottom of it) that the "Friends of the Players" hit on the idea of giving us a Celebration Dinner on our return.

There had been one supporter present in the audience who had travelled specially from London to be with us, but who did not let us know of his presence for fear of upsetting one of our number. It was Bob Yaxley.

A further very happy little memory of our stay in Bristol remains; our stroll together on a perfect Spring Sunday morning through the lovely gardens of Clifton Zoo, rested, relaxed and happy in each other's company. I remember that we re-cast "Dear Brutus" from the inmates—very unflattering to me, and I don't think Ernest or Bewsey came out of it very well either.

It was a tranquil little epilogue to our most exciting adventure of all, one which made for a rather special relationship between those of us who shared it that has lasted for the rest of our lives.

CHAPTER NINETEEN

FLYING HIGH

If there is one thing more boring than success it is being told about it.
Nevertheless, for the record:—
from the Western Gazette. 19.4.46.

SHERBORNE ENTERTAINS TROPHY WINNERS

"Sherborne's pride at the triumph of the Amateur Players in the drama
festival at the Theatre Royal, Bristol, when they carried off the Bristol
Guild of Players Shield with "Dear Brutus" took a tangible form on
Monday evening, when "Friends of the Players" entertained members
of the company at a Celebration Dinner. The performers and back-stage
personnel received small gifts as a token of the town's gratitude not
only for the success at the festival and for the grand entertainment
that the Company had provided locally, but for the help which has been
given to charitable organisations for many years.

Among the guests of honour were Mr. A. E. Scott-Piggott and Miss
Barbara Rogers (Chairman and Hon. Secretary of the Bristol Guild of
Players) who were welcomed by Brig.-Gen. R. L. Waller, (Chairman of
Sherborne Urban Council.) Gen. Waller took the opportunity of ex-
pressing on behalf of the townspeople, the great pride which was felt
at the success achieved, and he thanked the players and those behind
the scenes who had worked so hard to make it possible, the crowning
triumph after a long period of fine effort.

Mr. Scott-Piggott, in presenting the shield to Mr. Fred. B. Alcock,
said Bristol had always prided itself upon its standard of drama, but
at the festival along came a group from Sherborne. They came and
they conquered, and he congratulated them with all his heart upon
a perfect performance. When the final curtain came down on "Dear
Brutus", leading judges in Bristol said, "If any company can beat this
performance there is something wrong with our judgement" and they
had been proved absolutely right. The company had gone so far as
to make a convert out of one of the greatest anti-Barrie critics in
England—that was the measure of the play's success."

My own speech, reported at length, expressed doubts about the acclaim,
and anxiety for the future. The "Hedda Gabler" company, suffering illness,
had been only two marks behind us and at that, Press opinion had not been
unanimous. There was now the danger that we might consider ourselves to
be good, and the difficulty that it would be expected of us. The one great
reward for being declared winners was that almost certainly we would be
invited to return to Bristol in 1947.

So much for what was said. Much more though for my own private wonder. On a summer evening twelve years earlier, sitting on the stone steps at the back of the Church Hall, with Alan Cobham's Air Circus going on overhead, I had made a resolve to try, however ineffectively, to bring a professional approach to an amateur show, and tonight I had seen achievement generously acknowledged. The Bristol Trophy, with "Amateur Players of Sherborne" inscribed, spoke for our standards and Gen. Waller's tribute, spoken for the town, acclaimed the outcome of our work, artistic and financial. Those twelve years had brought the Players a long way, and—surprising thought—I alone had covered the whole course.

But for how much longer? Due to Brookie's dynamic management, business at Lloyds had grown dramatically and with it had come my promotion to the status of Accountant, which, whilst keeping me in Sherborne for a time, was a rung on the ladder. My interview in Lombard Street had surprised me, for after making such a poor start in my career and having gained my A.I.B. so late, I had never seen myself as a prospective Manager. Brookie had other ideas though, and I know it gave him, pleasure to see me climb eventually to my fourth managerial appointment. (I even sought his advice before accepting that, too!)

Brookie was to die in 1958, just before he was to have retired, and the large congregation, which (to the surprise of some) filled the Abbey to pay last tributes, included Lloyds Bank men from all over the Country, who at some time in their careers had been fortunate enough to benefit from his influence. He had been Treasurer to the Players until 1950, when he was succeeded by Mervyn Davies. It is a nice thought for me that the A.P.S. bank account is kept at Lloyds to this day. We had sprung from there and once—in "The Scarlet Pimpernel"—the name of every member of the staff, from Manager to Junior, appeared in the programme in one capacity or another.

With the years and the Players' increasing autonomy it was inevitable and beneficial that some old ideas should change, but we still aimed primarily to make money. It now came easily, for recent publicity brought invitations to take "Dear Brutus" to a number of towns and we cheerfully started out on our second tour of the play, this time to Stoke, Shaftesbury, Blandford (disasters there—the glass roof of the Corn Exchange and the light evening combined to ruin the darkened opening—and Joy dropped her biscuit). Gillingham and perhaps elsewhere—I have forgotten. Most of the schools we appeared at had been built at about the same time and to a common design, so we had no great problems, so far as I remember, in staging. We could now find Seymours some relief occasionally in moving scenery and props, partly from Gerald Brett and also from Jim Myers who had come to Sherborne with the Ordnance Depot in Marston Road, bringing with him his wife Dorothy (a good musician and one of the original Ivy Benson Band).

The Company always travelled in one of Seager's coaches driven either by Bert Poole or Alwyn Lugg both whom soon found themselves part of the show as scene shifters (in which they were experienced from Carlton days), and with special responsibilities in minding our mobile bar and finding the local fish and chip shop.

Wherever we went we found a warm welcome and full houses. It was all tremendous fun for us, enhanced by the knowledge that we were earning quite big profits. For this we had to thank, in great part, the indefatigable Mrs. Mary Morling and her Dioceson Welfare Committees, who could be depended upon to provide a strong local organisation in each place we visited.

This "tour" carried us through to the early summer and must have been one of the happiest, carefree periods we had known together. We had a successful show which we knew backwards, both as to mounting and acting, and we never wearied of it. We were doing much good, doing what we liked doing best, with those we best liked doing it. Of all ages and from diverse backgrounds, we were a most united band of good friends, whose pleasure in each other's company never dimmed. But like most good things . . .

Margery married and left us, to be succeeded as Secretary and Business Manager, by Meg Hulme. Crock set out for Australia to be replaced by Jim Myers, and it was time to plan the Autumn Production for the benefit of the Church Hall, as promised.

* * * * *

As a sequel, more or less, to "Quiet Wedding", "Quiet Weekend" was a certain box-office draw, better in fact than we anticipated. We arranged to put on five performances in Sherborne, including for the first time two evening shows on the Saturday, at 5 p.m. and 8 p.m. But it was not enough; our Western Gazette advert carried an "All Reserved Seats Sold" note and I had to apologise in the last night curtain speech to the many people turned away at the door. The following week, the Gazette chided us:—" The number of extra performances given this year still failed to satisfy the demand, and the Company will have to consider seriously having a full week's run for future productions".

The author, Esther McCracken, presented nearly all the Royd household from "Quiet Wedding" again and we found nearly all the same actors for the parts. But there was one most significant alteration. Meg Hulme was needed for a new character, so Bewsey (as Jim Brent) had to be found another wife, and she materialised in the person a charming young ex-W.R.N.S. Officer, and Secretary to the Headmaster of Sherborne School, Stella Thurgood. "There is a tide in the affairs of men—".

There was another important newcomer also. For some reason Bewsey could not appear on one night and for the first time in our history we played an understudy, Jack Dodge, of whom the "Western" said, "he won golden opinions. No doubt more will be seen of him in future productions." True too. Jack was to prove one of the keenest sponsors for the formation of a "proper" Society when the time came and in turn became its Chairman. Along the way he put in some good performances and much hard work in organisation.

Our Black Gang at this time was at its strongest technically, for in addition to Jim Myers and our usual band of enthusiasts it now included both Jack Lugg and Cyril Copp (Builders and Decorators). The result was a very "solid" set with, for the first time, a full ceiling with rafters.

For music, we had the services—free—of the new Blackmore Vale Light Orchestra, directed by Wilby Shaw (still a good friend) and including Mrs. Myers.

"Quiet Weekend" is remembered with embarrassment for my own dismally bad performance in it and with amusement for Bunter's struggles, night after night, with the line, "A bath in this house is an event and an adventure". All in all, I believe we provided an amusing evening for our packed houses and we certainly achieved our object in helping the Church Hall.

At the customary last-night ceremony our new Business Manager, Meg Hulme handed a cheque for £200 "on account" to Canon Lovett, and in thanking the Players the Vicar recalled that many of the other improvements effected in the Hall had been due to their efforts. Our programme note proudly boasted that previous "Gifts to Charitable Causes now exceed £1200". The total was increased still further from "the entire proceeds" of the tour to Stoke-under-Ham, Castle Cary and Sturminster Newton during the next ten days. In the end it all added up to a great deal of money given away and nothing kept back . . . for the very last time.

I will not admit to any deliberate ulterior motive in what happened next, but I cannot deny that it suited my purpose to yield to pressure and abandon the idea of "giving it all away". From all sides came arguments that we should build up reserves, in which I saw no virtue at all, nor any good purpose in keeping money in the bank; but for several reasons I would welcome unlimited funds to stage a production on a more lavish scale than ever before. If I had my way, our next play would do great business, but would barely cover expenses—just like the old Operatic Society which I had criticized so harshly in the past!

For one thing, it might well be my last production for the Players. I had already been sent to manage Lloyds, Gillingham for a short period in an emergency and it now seemed reasonably certain that I would gain my first Board Appointment soon, but before the move came there was one play I dearly longed to stage. It had caught my imagination as a wonderful piece of theatre, a producer's dream—but it was too expensive if we were aiming to help a cause.

There could be no better choice of play for the next Bristol Festival and the specialised audience we would find there; nor a play better suited to performance in the Theatre Royal, for it concerned life in the theatre of Shakespeare's day, telling of The Lord Chamberlain's Men, of the opening of The Globe and the first performance of "Twelfth Night"—but costumes and scenery alone would cost the earth.

There could be no better play either in which to give Joy her big chance and this was the greatest temptation of all. I shall never know whether at this time it really was Joy's one burning desire to make the stage her career, or whether my own enthusiasm was pushing her, discounting doubts about her stamina for such a tough profession and ignoring the way of life it would entail. I saw only her talent and of that there was no question. She had proved it again in "Quiet Weekend", playing Miranda, a winning little part (created by Glynis Johns) which gave her her first love scene.

But how to get started? There was no possibility of affording R.A.D.A.: Ronald Russell, who ran Bristol's Little Theatre Company, (of which my cousin Kathleen had once been a member) might have a student leaving in three months but she might stay on; Barbara Burnham at Salisbury Arts Theatre might have a vacancy for a student after Christmas. It was all very depressing, but no doubt about it, a success in a long and difficult leading role with attendant publicity in Bristol might induce a change of mind in either Mr. Russell or Miss Burnham. We asked nothing better, and here was a golden opportunity in just the right play.

But . . . thirty-one speaking parts, some making big demands on amateur actors; expensive costumes with elaborate changes and all "to special order"; a wealth of music off stage and on, vocal and instrumental, some specially composed by Herbert Menges, some traditional Elizabethan; a complicated production job, with crowd scenes, "simultaneous" dialogue and, visually, a difficult climax:—Richard Burbage's bed-chamber in Shore-ditch to be converted into "Orsino's Palace" during the action of the play; specialised furniture and properties (including a full-size four-poster bed). Finally, a set impossible to build ourselves, demandng three levels, a full staircase up to a gallery and two upstairs exits. All to be easily transport-able. And this for a play which had never enjoyed a West End success.

Yet there was no real doubt in my mind. This was not a time when we recognised difficulties or doubted our abilities. All we needed was money to spend and I knew we could take it with almost any play we cared to stage, for we were flying high. No need now to rely on a popular box-office attrac-tion; no need to seek support for a good cause. The Players were now a draw on their own account and although there is nothing to feel very proud of in using that for utterly selfish aims, I fear that is as it was.

We would approach what would probably be my final production on a strictly commercial basis. For the first time the Company would not be asked to meet their own personal expenses; the show would pay our way to Bristol and we would mount it handsomely, better than ever before. Costing would best be done on my own in the first place, avoiding committee meetings as long as possible!

So to Lugg and Copp, Builders and Decorators.

CHAPTER TWENTY

"SPRING 1600"

In the year 1600, Ann, daughter of William Byrd, "the father of English Music", ran away on the eve of her wedding to an unattractive musician, Master John Kynaston, and journeyed from Ongar, in Essex, to London, disguised, for reasons of safety, as a boy.

In the year 1600, ladies did NOT appear upon the stage.

In the year 1600, William Shakespeare's new comedy, "Twelfth Night" opened the Globe Theatre on the South Bank of the Thames, following, it is said, a private performance before Queen Elizabeth. At this, Viola was brilliantly portrayed by an unknown boy actor, Jack Beeston, who disappeared after that one performance and was hastily replaced by Perkyn of the Queen's Chapel.

From this blend of history, legend and imagination Emlyn Williams had made the play which above all others I wanted to produce. Only once before, in the case of "Night Must Fall" had I felt this compulsive urge on reading a play, and then I had been made to wait eighteen months for the chance. Not this time however, for "Spring 1600" had been around in one form or another for over ten years.

The original version, written in 1933, was produced at the Shaftesbury Theatre by John Gielgud, with lavish settings and costumes by Motley. Alas, despite the brilliant idea, intriguing situation, witty dialogue and rich romance, it failed. Too long and too complicated—even with cuts totalling forty-five minutes made by the author after the first night.

During the next decade Mr. Williams enjoyed many great successes both as actor and author and might well have put "Spring 1600" out of mind, Great plays, some of the best of the thirties and forties—"Night Must Fall", "The Corn is Green" (partly autobiographical), "The Morning Star" (his war play), "The Light of Heart", (containing surely the most moving declaration of love in the modern theatre), "The Wind of Heaven"; and others, lesser perhaps, but all fine theatre. Yet the idea for "Spring 1600" survived, and in 1945 Mr. Williams himself produced its "final version" (his words) after much re-writing and revision, for the "Company of Four" at the Lyric, Hammersmith and on tour, with Miss Jessica Spencer and Mr. Andrew Cruickshank in the leading roles.

This version of the play was published and for me it was still too long and too complicated. So for the first time, though not, I fear, the last I committed the sin of tinkering with the text, merging the two scenes in Act II, thus excising a short episode which I thought irrelevant. And the ease with which this could be done pointed up the play's one shortcoming, its lack of incident. The colourful characters, piquant situation, the air of authenticity about the theatrical, "behind the scenes" life of the Lord Chamberlain's Men all combined to hold one's interest closely, but despite all the excitement, nothing very much actually happens and I knew at the outset where the emphasis would have to lie if we were to give the play impact.

Casting presented no difficult choices, for we would need everyone we could find! Nearly every member of the black gang had a part to play also. Even Cyril Copp was roped in—not unwillingly either—to play Master Kynaston in the first scene. He was only called upon to snore audibly at appropriate moments but, like the rest of us, he took it all very seriously and conscientiously.

Ernest Hulme manfully tackled the role of Richard Burbage, "The Master" for whom Shakespeare was later to write Lear, Hamlet and Othello, so it fell to him to show us how the greatest actor of the day behaved in private life. The several professional opinions offered all differed about it and Ernest's version is as likely to have been correct as any other. In the event his performance was no less than a tour de force. His wife Meg played his wife Winifred, the stage manager to the Company—"in bed early for tonight whilst Richard is in bed late from last night so that for a brief while our paths cross and we may renew our marriage vows".

Much of the humour lay with Bunter as Thomas Day, who had earlier created "Juliet" and Charles Gillingham (a newcomer and a great find) as Ned Pope, "famous for his older dames". Fred Forrest played Henry Cordell, one of Burbage's favourite actors and a close friend of Shakespeare. Jack Dodge was Will Kempe, the first of the Shakespearean clowns, Bill Brown was Augustin Phillips who, thirty years earlier had been the Country's leading actor.

And so on. All "Lord Chamberlain's Men". All making heavy demands on the amateur actors who dared to portray these picturesque characters of the early English stage.

One further member of this distinguished company merits special mention. Appearing on the programme only as "A Visitor", he provided Mervyn Davies with a part which, considering it comprised only a single line of five words, must be unique in its effect. The make-up took Mervyn hours, but he perfected it and was instantly recognised when he appeared at the very end of the first act.

"Is Master Burbage at home?"—and off. Then, from the Company's new boy actor, "Who was that?", and the reply, "Only a fellow that writes plays —William Shakespeare."

It was Mervyn's big moment and he was not even on stage to enjoy it, but it made a great curtain line.

To play the romantic lead and provide the "happy ever after" ending, Stanley McKay of Foster's School staff joined the Company and in him the Players found a good friend who eventually became Chairman and a

Producer.

"Spring 1600" was the only play in which I was ever able to have my whole family taking part. Judy, aged twelve, joined her sister to play "A Boy", with a line or two of her own and Doris was well enough again to come in as Mother Harelip, Burbage's one-time nurse and now fortune-teller to the Company. It was a tiny part and once more, without obtruding in any way, Doris showed us what can be achieved with only a line or two. Three adjudicators commented upon "Spring 1600" in turn and each one singled out Doris's performance for special praise. It delighted me, and the memory still does. It was alas, to be her last part.

Nor was this the sum of the family involvement in the play, although I was unaware of it at the time. "Spring 1600" is a trifle short on glamour, but it has got Lady Coperario, and in the hands of Elizabeth Dyke this patron of the Arts cum wealthy courtesan fairly glittered. Grand in manner, gorgeous in appearance and caressing a pet monkey, she was attended by a large blackamoor called Nebuchadnezzar strumming a guitar. And to play the part of the blackamoor came a sailor home from the sea, Jim Saunders. Whatever possessed him to take up amateur theatricals I shall never know— or should I? It was, I believe, his first and his last appearance on any stage, but for good measure he played two parts, the other being a Manservant to stand at Joy's right hand at the very beginning of the play and speak the opening line. To be perfectly fair to my son-in-law, whatever his intentions in joining the Players—and I don't think it was the urge to act—he did very well in both parts.

Casting simply and easily done, the knottier problems had to be faced and, as so often, they proved worse in prospect than when tackled quietly. The production work was intricate and did scare me at first, but taking it very slowly, page by page, I found I was building quite a workable prompt-book. It soon became clear that I should need help, for so much of the stage action was in fact reaction to what was going on off-stage. Crowds cheering or jeering, marching or dancing, much music, formal and impromptu, and all "live" where possible. So Bewsey was appointed "Off-Stage Effects Director" and he had a busy time.

Far from dismissing my rather elaborate plot for the set as impracticable, Lugg and Copp, unhampered by any expense limit, produced a beauty. It may not have been of traditional construction, but with two off-stage ladders to the "upstairs" exits opposing the on-stage staircase and gallery, and the flats standing just free, it stood remarkably firm and steady. Doors with heavy wooden latches and a big latticed window looking out on the Thames with its shipping had to be made, but we could use the frames of the fireplace and main arch with the steps from the "Dear Brutus" interior. Skilfully painted in beams and plaster, cracked, with patches of damp, it had just the right atmosphere and formed the background of what would prove to be a most satisfying stage picture.

The highly specialised furniture and properties presented problems, (Here were some we could not borrow from the Forrests)—but Lugg and Copp solved the most difficult one by making us a magnificent four-poster bed out of all sorts of odds and ends, including old picture-frame mouldings. Ernest, who had to sleep in it for twenty minutes, was loud in complaint, but it looked splendid.

For the remainder we turned to a couple, the last of those to enter our story who would play a significant role in making the Players "legitimate" when the time came, Ken and Joan Miller. Actually they were not quite new to us. Joan had understudied Eizabeth Dyke in "Dear Brutus" and Ken had helped with properties for "Quiet Weekend". He was a tremendous enthusiast in all that he undertook, and now he and Joan together worked very hard with invention and ingenuity to provide us with furniture and properties of authenticity which again did wonders for the finished picture.

So did the costumes. By the time all was done, the lady at Nathans who had charge of our show was an old friend and it is to my shame that I have forgotten her name. "Spring 1600" was not a stock production, so we had to study details together—a "Twelfth Night" Olivia costume for a 6ft. man was one item to stir the imagination!

So far, all in my own good time—an orderly preparation. Then, suddenly, utter panic. To suit the Old Vic Company the Bristol Festival was to be brought forward from April to the week commencing March 10th, seven weeks away. For many reasons it was almost essential that we get the Sherborne production on first and it was a great relief to find that with Mr. Steele's help and some changes in other bookings we could have the Church Hall for the week March 3-8, opening on Wednesday 5th. Six weeks! And worse to come.

John Wilkins reappeared with an appeal—more a summons really—to take part in the B.D.L. Festival, now revived after the War, at Summerleaze School, Yeovil on Wednesday, March 12th. We had been allotted Saturday 15th to play at the Theatre Royal, Bristol, so it was lunacy to do anything other than decline the Yeovil Festival. Yet, as Area Finalists in 1939, we felt some sort of duty to put in an appearance if it were humanly possible. Every single available Player was involved in "Spring 1600", so there was no question of raising a second company and the only offer we could make would be an extract from the play. We would have the costumes on hand anyway and, if we could assemble and dismantle the bed in time, we could make do in a curtain setting. Yes, we would enter the B.D.L. Festival, and the Players were to forget all about it until three days beforehand!

There was no single forty-minute extract which would make sense, let alone acceptable entertainment, but I believed a good little play in two scenes could be made, taking from Act I ("The Atheists Tragedy" rehearsal) the recruiting of the new boy actor and from Act III the final preparation for the opening of "Twelfth Night".

The first thing was to obtain permission from Margery Vosper, Mr. Williams' agent, to perform "Excerpts from "Spring 1600". There was no difficulty about this, nor any restriction, so I went to work. It was not just a matter of cutting, for although I used no words but the author's, a good deal of transplanting had to be done. Act II, for instance, although not much used, contained many gems not to be missed.

Burbage: (Picking up a loose sheet fallen from a script)
What have we here . . . "To die, to sleep; to sleep, perchance to . . . " Hm . . . some idea of Will's, may come in useful.

And the final lines of Act II—
Burbage: It came to me that beyond all this there may be something more . . . that all of us players and playwrights, Hemyng, Kempe, Nashe, Shakespeare, Tourneur, that in the end, we may not all be forgot. For beyond us there may grow a shadow that may steal into a majesty over the whole world. I listened, straining my ears. And I thought I heard, far away . . . a fluttering of immortality . . .

For years I have treasured a beautifully decorated manuscript of that last speech, given me by Violet Upshall (Grizzy Frost in the play) later in 1947 as a leaving present.

When all was done we had a cohesive compact one-act play, conveying, I believe, the essence of the author's intention. The work took longer than I had expected and I had to devote all my spare time from our rehearsals to it, because the script had to be submitted well in advance of the performance. Right or wrong, I liked it.

Meanwhile, work on the full play went ahead urgently and in some adversity. The severity of that early 1947 winter is a matter of history; we suffered a good deal of illness in the company, it was bitterly cold and power cuts were long and frequent. At last Mr. and Mrs. Collins had to tell us they could no longer heat our rehearsal room at the Mermaid for lack of fuel, so those of us living nearest took it in turns to get there early carrying a bucket of coal for a small fire. But our spirits never dropped; we were a cheerful crowd and it all went forward with enthusiasm. In particular I marvelled at the patience and good nature of the many "bit" players slogging through hours of what must have been drudgery as we learned to give point to the spells of simultaneous dialogue. Somehow, during continuous movement and through a jumble of words, each one of a crowd of sixteen had to be on his allotted square to deliver his allotted line at a precise second, so that the whole came across as a sensible flow of conversation, clearly audible above the rest and apparently casual. It was a complicated business which, I am sorry to say, I kept getting wrong, and we had to go over it again and again. They were wonderfully good about it and eventually it grew into an effective piece of work.

With details of the Bristol Festival came the shock news that it was to be non-competitive. I could hardly complain, for from the stage of the Theatre Royal I had publicly stated my view that the competitive element did little for the spirit of Festival, but we had relished the challenge and now took a dim view of the organisers' decision, made just when the Trophy had left the City of Bristol for the first time. In the event we mounted our precious shield on the back of the set, only relinquishing it after our play was done.

The adjudicator was to be Mr. Edward Stanley, and the week's plays: "While The Sun Shines" (John Bennett's Thirteen Players aiming at amusement only), "The Corn Is Green", "Much Ado About Nothing", (Bristol Shakespeare Society), "Claudia", "Watch On The Rhine" (Hartly Hodder Players—Drama School actors, some "appearing by arrangement with Hedley Goodall", the "class" company of the week), and "Spring 1600".

Our welcome, particularly from the Bristol Press, was in strong contrast to the previous year. Gone was the "Country Comes to Town" approach. Now it was, "Sherborne, last year's winners are bringing an elaborate production with a huge cast and special scenery" (Evening World). Clearly much was expected of us.

Earlier in the same week, at Yeovil, we would find ourselves in competition with five other companies in the B.D.L, Festival, playing the shortened version of "Spring 1600" after only three rehearsals, starting the day after the Sherborne production's last night.

With final rehearsals and five performances in the week before that, it all added up to the tightest schedule we have ever attempted and nothing but our very best would do. There was too much at stake.

No worries though. No time for worry. No hitches in administration or organisation. And no tribute could be too generous to Meg Hulme, our new Business Manager for her handling of the complicated arrangements. Left to herself, without the cushion of committee decisions to fall back on, she accepted responsibility and dealt with all the tasks and problems in her own way, calmly and efficiently. In short, Meg really did manage our business and we were incredibly fortunate to have her in the job at this time.

So we approached our Dress Rehearsal in confident mood. Advance bookings for this comparatively unknown costume play ("death to the Box-Office") had broken records, our new policy of having two evening performances on the Saturday (5 p.m. and 8.30) had paid off. On Sunday the costumes had been tried and approved. On Monday the set had been put up in time for early photo calls, and then Bill Hall and I settled down to light the show. For me this was the crucial bit.

For the first time in our history we had decided to dispense entirely with battens and floats, using only directional lighting with support from an A.A. Flood or two. All our spotlights had to go out to the front of the house, so for the spot bars we had to run up quite a bill with Strand Electric.

The author required that the main scene should open on a tableau. I had seen the idea prove excitingly effective years before in "She Stoops to Conquer" with Michael Redgrave and, I think Diana Churchill, when each act opened with a picture based on a Rowlandson watercolour. What I now had in mind was something like a Hogarth print, a picture motionless, but brimming with coarse vitality and energetic action suddenly arrested. Easy as an idea, but in truth neither Bill nor I had the technical experience to bring it off short of hours of experiment and much error. We sorely tried the patience of the actors who had to wait, each in his place, for what must have seemed an age, whilst we "placed" the lights, changing colours and intensity until we stumbled on the right combination.

But we all got our reward. At the Dress Rehearsal on Tuesday that tableau, slotted correctly into the action of the play, brought us one of those very rare theatrical moments not to be forgotten.

The first short scene, stiffly formal and static, played before a traverse, had closed to the sound of distant church bells and a choir practising for the wedding tomorrow, and the bride's plan to run away already laid. The lights died away with the sounds, but the ensuing subdued, darkened quiet was suddenly shattered by a strident trumpet call heralding the change of mood and tempo, and up swelled the lights, delicately balanced to illumine and colour our picture. Even I, who had strived so hard for the effect, gasped with the others who saw it now. Here was the very "painting" I had dreamed of—and much much more effective than anything I could have hoped to achieve.

Dirt and disorder everywhere; but colour, and that atmosphere of tarnished glamour which belongs so especially to "theatricals". Richard Burbage's bedchamber, cluttered with the belongings of a man of untidy and extravagant habits—wine bottles, play-house posters, theatrical costumes, goblets, helmets, manuscripts, musical instruments, brooms, books, dirty plates, utensils, logs of wood, dog's bones. Most prominent a four-poster bed with garish curtains; next, a wooden stage throne (once richly coloured, now shabby), clothes-baskets piled with all sorts of costumes, an old set of virginals, empty barrels used as tables and seats. Hung between the bedpost and balcony, a clothes-line with kerchiefs and tights.

"The room is littered with people as it is with objects, for a rehearsal is in progress, conducted by Winifred Burbage, squatting in the dishevelled bed, clad in a voluminous nightgown, munching a chunk of bread. Henry Condell holds the stage, struck in a declamatory pose, draped in a not-too-clean curtain. Ned Pope, plump and effeminate, tricked out in velvet, sits on the throne, one leg crossed elegantly over the other. Will Kempe, disillusioned and solemn—the perfect clown—is perched on a barrel, a grubby part in one hand, a half-eaten apple in the other. Old Augustin Phillips is crouched over a bass viol. Thomas Day adorns the virginals, correcting music. Young Salathiel Pavey is practising contortions. George Pearce and Ben Cook play at marbles. Mother Harelip, tiny and incredibly dirty, leans over the balcony deep in thought, reading her own palm. Grizzy Frost is washing threadbare tights in a large pail."

There was our tableau, the author's directions obeyed to the letter, and I believe we did him justice. Rarely have I ever felt such satisfaction, and when after a long, long pause, the lights came up full and the action sprang to life—"Murder, Murder, Murder"—the glow remained. "Just wait". I thought. "Just wait till they see that tomorrow!" Really, I should have known better.

*　*　*　*　*

The worst power failure of the winter commenced at about 5 p.m. We didn't worry much at first, the lights would soon come on again—they usually did—but as one hour stretched to two, doubts began to arise, and soon after seven o'clock we were racking our brains as to the best thing to do if any of the audience were mad enough to arrive. Brookie favoured returning the ticket money and prepared to open the strong-room and cash safe—all the key-holders were on hand, himself, myself, Mervyn and Ruth Berry—but this was resisted, an instinctive reluctance to abandon the show. Then came the news that the lights had come on again in the northern end of the town, so we decided to go on waiting. The audience did arrive, nearly all carrying torches or lanterns—(we were not unaccustomed to getting about in the black-out). And slowly it dawned upon us that, lights or no lights, they expected to be entertained. We simply could not keep them waiting too long before doing something about it.

I can't think where all the hurricane lamps came from; six, perhaps more, which we stood or hung around the set, but I do remember that we knocked up Carters and Webbs for all the candles they would allow us, and that King's School boys in the back row were moved to the front with their torches and beseeched to hold them still.

There was some comfort in the fact that we were playing "Spring 1600" and not "While The Sun Shines". We did have a play capable of accepting primitive lighting and, here and there, even benefiting from it Thank heaven too that we were avoiding "canned" sound effects whenever possible. Our off-stage choir would have extra work to do!

The first spontaneous applause from a full house greeted the placing of some candles along the front of the stage to serve as footlights. There was going to be a show! And from then on we really could not go wrong. At about 8.15 p.m., quarter of an hour late, we rang up.

The footlights nearly all blew out in the draught as the curtain went up, so our first scene was illuminated by only the schoolboys' torches and two hurricane lamps held by hand on each side just behind the proscenium arch. It was just visible.

In the nick of time someone remembered that we couldn't dim out the scene and must drop the curtain. No church bells, but the choir "practised" all the harder. A longer wait than intended while the hurricane lamps were replaced, then the trumpet call. No "effects" record on tape, this, but a fine flourish from behind the stage played by a lad recruited from the Boys Brigade band, who today does so much for Sherborne Town's music, Cyril White.

As the curtain rose again, I was ready to weep for the lovely stage picture we had taken such pains to create. But no. For one thing the audience effectively stifled any regrets and for another I was myself too moved by the picture we did see. All eyes had by now become accustomed to the dim light, and were quite ready to accept the soft pools shed by lamps from within the picture itself, and the effect was something to wonder at. It may have been the absence of artificiality—no coloured beams from off stage, no unnatural shadows from unseen light sources—I don't know. Nor can I find the word for the unique quality our picture now possessed. Texture, perhaps or substance. It doesn't matter. The soft "oh's" from the house, breaking into applause is what counts. Applause such as we had never known on curtain-up before. It was music to us.

When we did get under way, and Jack Dodge had to make several attempts at his "Murder, Murder, Murder" before we could—it fell to Reg. Gregory (in his first year of many as our House Manager) to relight the footlights with a box of matches. Thereafter he posted himself on guard at one side, crossing in his best Sidesman's walk whenever necessary to replace a guttering candle. At his side the Fireman on duty kept sharply alert: The Police stayed mercifully away.

Whatever may have happened to the electricity supply, nothing dimmed the performance. Almost as if they relished the situation, the whole Company put the show over with a zest and an exhilarating air of enjoyment which crossed the footlights to great effect. Ernest, bless him, gave us all the bravura and style of The Master, but he also found a depth of tender emotion I had never known was in him. And Joy's performance? Next day I wrote to Bristol Old Vic begging that someone should see her act at the Theatre Royal next week. (There was no reply.)

Power restored, we could have our lighting effects on the second night and they did all we had hoped for, but I hated being told over and over again "It was better by lantern light, Fred!". For some time afterwards when "Spring 1600" was talked about, one would hear it said: "Ah, but I was there on the first night". It had certainly been one to remember.

With the show now running smoothly to the end of the week, I concentrated on preparing the one-act version for the first rehearsal on Sunday, realising that I had to have it absolutely cut and dried by then, for there would be no time for alteration. If we were to make anything of a showing in Yeovil on Wednesday, we would need a lot of luck.

But we were not short of well-wishers. In a delightful spontaneous gesture—a complete surprise for us—the Chairman of the Council, Mr. E. H. F. Dammers came on to the stage at the conclusion of the final Saturday performance to wish us—"the very best of good fortune in the coming events at Yeovil and Bristol. We are confident you will do the Town great credit". His following tribute, generously couched and generously echoed by our audience greatly encouraged us all and his words have been cherished . . .

*   *   *   *   *

At 11.30 next morning, seventeen of the cast, exactly half, met at the Wessex Club to read "Excerpts from Spring 1600" for the first time. It would all be quite simple; just a few cuts to be observed and some new cues to be learnt. The hard work lay with the stage staff—furniture, properties etc. to be sorted and separated for the shortened edition of the play, but much of this had been done already. So, sitting round the club committee room, relaxed and comfortable, we reeled it off with easy confidence a couple of times.

In fact, we were soon to discover we had been sitting much too comfortably; indeed, that we were far too casual about the whole thing.

The One-Act Festival had attracted six entries for the Preliminary, in two sessions, to be adjudicated by Mr. Maxwell Wray. Stage rehearsals were spread over two evenings of which we were allotted an hour on Monday, an arrangement that suited us well, for it would enable us to have a rest on Tuesday—our first evening off for a long time—and we needed it.

I would dearly like to forget the utter misery of that dreadful Monday rehearsal. I had no excuse: it had gone quite well when we had talked it through; we knew the Summerleaze stage, we had acted on it and knew it was small; yet as we tried to put the four-poster together and set the furniture and then move seventeen people around on it we saw it actually shrinking before our eyes. Some furniture had to go, which upset some moves, which upset some actors, who lost their lines and then their heads. Never was there such confusion—and to cap it all the fireplace fell in. I had failed to adjust some of the crossings to fit the cuts in dialogue: I had failed to allow even the minimum time for a costume change during the action; and I had failed to time it correctly—we would over-run the permitted forty minutes and be disqualified. In fact, I had messed it up, and the only possible course seemed to be to withdraw, or at best to play but not compete, and take our own time.

Meg and Ernest would have none of this however, and they rallied the remainder of the cast. I went home and sat up very late chopping off another five minutes and re-plotting the confused crossings. Then we all met at the Mermaid next evening and what was to have been a night off became about three hours of as hard and concentrated effort as we had known. When we had done, it still was not good, but it was better.

Next evening, playing last, we won the Festival. Yeovil Lit., second with "Where Three Ways Meet", were promoted with us to the Divisional Final. Third came Ilminster, with "Dark Brown".

Mr. Maxwell Wray who "liked the adaptation immensely" was complimentary to us, but he had some good words of advice too, and we listened carefully—there was something for nearly every one of us. And he went on to make much of the feat we were attempting:—"These people learnt the full play in seven weeks, gave five performances last week, rehearsed the shortened edition on Sunday for the first time, played it tonight and must now learn the full play again ready for production on Saturday at the Theatre Royal, Bristol". All beside the point, but, duly published, it was a good advertisement.

Finally, my "personal puff":—"I give great credit to anyone who can move such a large number of actors about so meaningfully on such a small stage."

If he had seen it on Monday!

*　*　*　*　*

Thursday. Back to the Mermaid and the full play. A relief to get back to the original cues and a relief also to find our experience in Yeovil had not impaired the production. In fact the reverse. Mr. Wray's comments were valuable, his criticism warranted time spent on some points, and his praise helped our assurance. A good rehearsal:—good enough to add a fair measure of confidence to the tingling excitement next morning when we saw Wild & White's van off with our scenery, props and costumes to the Theatre Royal, Bristol for the second time.

It had been intended that only a few of us, needed for the "get-in", would stay overnight, the remainder of the company travelling by coach in time for Dress Rehearsal at 3 p.m., but in the event quite a crowd of us gathered in the lounge of the Grand Hotel late on Friday night. Some had been to see "Watch On The Rhine" and were much impressed both by the acting and the adjudication. The Festival, it seemed, may have lost something in being non-competitive but it had gained status by now being "in association with the Arts Council of Great Britain". Again, Saturday was to be a "prestige" occasion, with all sorts of notabilities present, and we had

128

been selected for that night, not because we were last year's winners, but for our choice of play and the scale of production it entailed. "Spring 1600" was awaited "with special interest"—a weight of responsibility of which we were quite unaware as we sat round in a big circle chatting away happily late into the night.

That evening was marked for me by a coincidence. It seemed so strange, remembering the impact of "The Mikado" upon me at the age of fifteen and where it had led me, to find it here at The Hippodrome on the very eve of my biggest theatrical effort. Stranger still to be exchanging pleasantries at the bar of the Grand with Mr. Isidore Godfrey, D'Oyly Carte's distinguished musical director for so many years. Now in a lounge suit again and drinking a quiet draught bitter, he bore little resemblance to the disciplinarian of the orchestra pit whose eye was not easily forgotten by latecomers unwise enough to keep the overture waiting!

Mr. Godfrey was more than ready to join us, chat and "unwind", Entirely unassuming, he held us enthralled with his stories of life with D'Oyly Carte; the hardships of perpetual touring in this Country and abroad, the loss of home life, the need for constant rehearsal because audiences know the operas by heart—"One slip and there's a letter to The Times next day."

We did our share of talking too, for Mr. Godfrey was curious to know all about us and how we came to be, as he jokingly put it, "the opposition at the Royal tomorrow". He knew Sherborne, had met B. J. F. Picton and spoke of Rupert D'Oyly Carte's son who had been at the School. He appeared to be genuinely interested in us, asking almost wistfully about our families and jobs. In wishing us luck in our coming adventure he added, "As serious actors you appear to be getting the best of both worlds tomorrow—real involvement in the theatre without dependence upon it. I would say you've found the right recipe". Just then the professional and the amateur seemed not so many miles apart.

The right recipe. It may have been the wine talking, but it was a nice thought to take to bed. Nice too, to forget "Spring 1600" for a little.

* * * * *

Lugg and Copp were first at the Royal next morning and by the time I arrived our set was going up. Ernie Peppin greeted us like old friends. He had just taken possession of the Royal's fine new lighting console—it looked to me exactly like a cinema organ—but there had been little opportunity to show it off so far that week, and our opening tableau alone was enough to arouse his interest. With Bill Hall prompting him he went to work with a will and he lit our show like the master he certainly was.

Polly Smith and Doris were busy unpacking costumes, Bewsey and Jim Myers working on off-stage effects, the Millers on furniture and properties. There was little for me to do but sit in the front of the circle and watch it all going on, and from there some time during the morning I noticed a man with a sheaf of papers walk on to the stage for a word with Jack Orwood, the Stage Carpenter who was putting up the Royal's own traverse for us. The stranger appeared to be very interested in our set, walking round it, asking questions and exchanging a little good-natured badinage with Lugg and Copp before going on his way chuckling with amusement. Only later did I learn that he was Hugh Hunt, Director of The Old Vic. Heaven alone knows what Jack Lugg had been telling him! Jack Orwood's comment: "That's the first time he's been down here this week." A lucky break for us—if he had liked what he had seen.

As the day's work progressed, I was assailed by a growing sense of unease. Everything was going just a little too smoothly. The "get-in" completed, light-cues tried, the coach on time and everyone present, we walked through a trouble-free rehearsal and then all joined our families and friends for a light meal which Meg had laid on for us at a nearby restaurant. I think about fifty of us sat down together, and there was no mistaking the convivial party atmosphere. It worried me. Where were the nerves? Where the butterflies? I did spot that Joy had gone quiet and was not eating much, but . . . My attempt at a "Good Luck" pep talk—"It may be the last night for us, but it's the first for the customers" etc. was a hopeless flop. It was end of term, and I had lost contact.

The festive spirit became even more evident in the dressing-rooms, and as I went back alone to the Grand to change into my dinner jacket, I felt really very anxious. We were facing the crucial performance of the most difficult and complicated production we had ever attempted, before a discerning audience who, on our Bristol record, expected the best of us, with a public adjudication to follow . . . And the Company seemed bent on a night out!

Why not? We had success at Sherborne and Yeovil behind us; we knew the show well enough to romp through it; and there was no competition to lose. But in truth the past three weeks had ben a hard unremitting strain and we were all very tired. Tonight we needed all the concentration we could muster. We simply could not afford to get careless. Besides, things go wrong for me on the last night . . .

Round to the Foyer and the Circle Bar to meet Guild officials and V.I.P.'s arriving and greet our Sherborne supporters. Introductions, polite murmurs of goodwill, "Thank you, I hope you enjoy it" over and over again. And at last—the last possible moment—backstage once more. A word to the beginners already in position before the traverse, and on to the main set to fidget pointlessly with the furniture (as usual) during the National Anthem. Then to the Prompt Corner to ring up.

Of course—although it was a long time since I last thought of it—this play and this audience were made for each other. So far, sympathy had tended to side with Ann Byrd in thinking The Chamberlain's Men might be haberdashers, but not tonight. This crowd, mostly players themselves, were at one with Salathiel Pavey in his amazement that she had never heard of "the best actors in the world". Here, all the theatrical allusions and "in" jokes were seized upon knowingly from the very start. A good audience, provided we didn't crack.

Our tableau vivant, illuminated by a skilled professional using all the resources of the Royal, brought a response which thrilled us all. Even old Peppin, sitting at his "organ", grinned at me and muttered, "its got 'em", as he waited—(much too long I thought, but he probably judged aright)—before taking the lights on up to set the action going. And from then on, that's just how it felt. It was not only the ready laughter either; we could sense the sympathy at moments of emotional tension so tellingly built up by the author—as at the end of Ann's simple little "audition" song for instance. The play had indeed "got 'em", and by the time the "fellow who writes plays" arrived to bring down the Act I curtain, I was as cock-a-hoop as the rest.

With the end of the interval, flattering comments filtered back to us from the bars and with them, suddenly sobering me, the electrifying buzz that Hugh Hunt was in front. Mr. Hunt had been the subject of some criticism from the Guild of Players for his lack of interest in the Festival, which, it was said, he had completely ignored. Well, he was in tonight—and staying. *Pray God nothing happens to spoil it now.*

But it so nearly did. My Last-Night Bogy held off until within ten minutes of the final curtain. Then, (sparing the details) an accident with a hand-property led to a false exit, leaving Stanley McKay and Joy on stage, completely stranded. No lines, no plot, nowhere to go. It was an agonising dilemma, utterly unexpected, in which no prompter could help. Greatly to their credit they kept their heads and, ad libbing like mad, the actors some-how got the play back on course; but the fact remains that there are two pages of Act III which our Bristol audience have not seen yet! The gaffe and the embarrassment must have been observed, but may have been forgotten in all the to-do of the play's closing moments: the hasty improvisation of "Orsino's Palace", the entry of Queen Elizabeth with her Courtiers, and finally the opening words of "Twelfth Night", "If music be the food of love . . ." the curtain descending through the line, the music swelling up.

We had a truly great reception which, with the ensuing congratulations, was more than we deserved, for it had not been the best we could give. Cele-brations had commenced too soon, leading almost inevitably to loss of concentration, some untidiness and a near disaster. I was dismayed, which in all the elation around me seemed absurd; all the more so when it came to Mr. Edward Stanley's Critical Analysis.

Describing the play as most difficult, he congratulated the company on their courage in undertaking its presentation. "The art of production means the fusing of all theatrical elements, and in the Sherborne play there is ample evidence of the fullest dramatic influence on the audience, a very considerable achievement." Saying the crowd scenes were worthy of the highest praise, Mr. Stanley spoke of "magnificent individual teamwork" (—nothing could have pleased me more, for it exactly expressed all we had aimed at).

Ernest, "with a large and difficult part", was vigorous and firm, but "perhaps more flamboyant than befitted the greatest actor of the day." (A direct contradiction of Mr. Wray's comment at Yeovil). He won praise for the temperamental outbursts, the vision of immortality for playwrights and players, and for the sudden tenderness when he found his star boy was a girl.

Elizabeth Dyke, as Lady Coperario, was credited with "one of the high spots of the evening" and there were many other compliments. Voice production 99% good. The play looked "simply splendid", and one of the biggest achievements was "the magnificent set".

Somewhere, amongst it all:—"Ann Byrd was played with charm and vigour, with many subtle touches and finesse. Ann was lovely and she was moving, with a rare and quite beautiful personality". But the best compliment of all was yet to come. A brief message to the dressing-room—Mr. Hunt would like to see Miss Alcock.

Afterwards, everyone was very generous, leaving us in no doubt that we had more than maintained our standing in Bristol. Privately I was a little sad to be told that in the general opinion of the critics "Spring 1600" had outdone "Dear Brutus".

Back home again, rather pleased with ourselves, we looked happily to see what nice things the Bristol papers had to say about us on Monday . . . Nothing. Not a word. Every other play had been reviewed the following day, but for some reason we were ignored.

That is, until Thursday when some notice had to be taken. The morning paper, Western Daily Press, had it first:—

FROM SHERBORNE TO JOIN THE OLD VIC

Miss Joy Alcock, whose striking performance in "Spring 1600" etc. etc. . . . has been engaged by Mr. Hugh Hunt to join the Old Vic Company for next season . . . Mr. Hunt said, "I was much impressed. I think she will become an actress of quality" . . .

The Evening Post:—

The Old Vic's Director happened to be at the Theatre Royal last Saturday when Miss Alcock etc. etc. . . . . The engagement is an exceptional one. Whilst playing with the Company, Miss Alcock will take part of the course at the Old Vic Theatre School.

In August 1947 Joy became a member of the Bristol Old Vic Company. Our blackamoor, Nebuchadnezzar, thought it was a rotten idea.

CHAPTER TWENTY-ONE

EXIT

We had not yet seen quite the end of "Spring 1600". With three weeks in which to polish up the shortened version, we approached the B.D.L. Divisional Final pretty sure of ourselves. It was staged in Yeovil on the 12th April, so we had the advantage of knowing the cramped conditions from recent experience and I think we rather fancied our chances of being back in Bristol again before long for the Area Final.

But we had reckoned without "Everyman". Bristol W.E.A. Players, notable absentees from the Theatre Royal Festival presented the premiere of a modern version of the mediaeval morality play "The Summoning of Everyman", made for them by Herbert W. Payne who also produced it and acted the part of Confession. And it was great. Beautifully staged on two levels, with a fine stairway, rostra and an imposing Cross, delicately lit, and acted by a cast of sixteen with a stark simplicity that conveyed utter conviction, it was most moving. Before it was halfway through I felt it made the rest of us look tawdry.

This was not everyone's opinion—there were some objections to the modern treatment of its deeply religious theme in a secular entertainment—but the facts speak for themselves—"Everyman" went on to win the Western Area Final and then to London to be placed second in the National Final at the Scala. It was later broadcast. The play was published and rightly took its place in the library of modern drama.

All this is relevant to our story (and our self-esteem!) for only one reason. In making his final placings at Yeovil, Mr. Frank Harwood, the Adjudicator described the W.E.A. play as "Epoch making". Then he said this:—"A close second with their presentation of an excellent adaptation, Sherborne. It is almost a split hair of difference between that and "Everyman". As an excerpt, "Spring 1600" is the best I have seen . . .". So near. Yet it would have been a dreadful injustice if "Everyman" had not gone forward to the fame it was to know.

Finally, my "personal puff" again:—"He is well on the way to being a producer of considerable stature." Wrong actually. I was on the way to being a Bank Manager.

Banking, and those awful attendant treasureships etc. won in the end, but there still lay ahead some ten years or so of active interest in amateur theatre:—

At Swindon, with an eager group of young people who have remained friends ever since. There we won a Festival with "Everyman" and later performed it in Church. (Daughter Judy as a lovely but very matter-of-fact, down-to-earth Angel).

In London, with Lloyds Bank D.S., playing at the Scala and Fortune Theatres. "Shop Window" theatricals this; everything bought and paid for by the Bank—we were not allowed even to do our own make-up.

At home in Harrow, with the Belmont Players, more friends for life, a gallant, happy little band, boundless in ambition and enthusiasm, rehearsing in each other's sitting-rooms, making scenery in garages and lofts. We borrowed props from the Old Vic (thanks to Bunter, then their Stage Manager) and curtains from Lloyds Bank Head Office (They were made from blue copper-bag material). Here Judy played her first lead, in "Death Takes a Holiday".

On to Gloucester, producing first for the Mynd Players and then for four years with the long-established and wealthy G.O.D.S. (finding myself committee bound again—and almost liking it!)

But those were other times, other places. Our story must end here, in 1947.

Yes, I know . . . Too many superlatives, too much success-story, too many nicest people, too much heart-on-the-sleeve. But, you see, looking back from a dusty shelf labelled three-score-years-and-ten, one is apt to remember the peaks, and nearly all of those in my life, the events and the relationships which have most affected me, are chronicled here. It is no small matter to me that when, after twenty years, I had to leave Sherborne to earn my living elsewhere, I could take with me the echo of Mr. Dammers' words on the last night of "Spring 1600":—

"The Players have done so much for Sherborne in so many ways. It would be so much a poorer place without them".

* * * * *

Extract from the Minutes of a General Meeting on the 25th November, 1948—**Constitution.**

It was unanimously agreed that the Society shall be called:—

AMATEUR PLAYERS OF SHERBORNE

Elected

President—Mr. W. J. Cordy   Chairman—Mr. M. M. Welcher
Hon. Sec.—Mrs. M. Hulme   Hon. Treas.—Mr. F. H. Brooks
Publicity—Mr. W. J. E. Brown   Technician—Mr. W. J. Hall

together with Mr. B. B. Dyke, Mr. K. Miller, Mr. J. Dodge.

It is someone else's story now.